DISCOVERING ODIA CULTURE
(A Few Intimate Experiences)

DISCOVERING ODIA CULTURE
(A Few Intimate Experiences)

Bhagyalipi Malla

Translated from Odia by
Urmishree Bedamatta

BLACK EAGLE BOOKS
2019

BLACK EAGLE BOOKS

7464 Wisdom Lane
Dublin, OH 43016
E-mail: info@blackeaglebooks.org
Website: www.blackeaglebooks.org

First International Edition Published by
BLACK EAGLE BOOKS, 2019

DISCOVERING ODIA CULTURE
(A Few Intimate Experiences)
by Bhagyalipi Malla

Translated by **Urmishree Bedamatta**

Copyright of original © **Bhagyalipi Malla**
Copyright translation © **Urmishree Bedamatta**

All rights reserved. No part of this publication may be reproduced, stored in a retrieval system, or transmitted, in any form or by any means, electronic, mechanical, photocopying, recording or otherwise without the prior permission of the publisher.

Cover: **Ramakant Samantaray**
Interior Design: Ezy's Publication

ISBN: 978-1-64560-049-7 (Paperback)
Library of Congress Control Number: 2019956169

Printed in United States of America

Introduction

Going through these short pieces, essentially written as columns for a newspaper, I found myself on an exciting cultural journey. The *osha, brata, pala, nata* etc. as described by the author are indelible expressions of Odia life and experience. Not very long ago, it was considered beneath oneself to even discuss the 'little tradition'. It was in 1831 with the establishment of Finnish Literature Society that the scholarly community took notice and the path was paved for in-depth study and research of local customs, rites and rituals. In India, in late nineteenth century, of course, there were attempts made by British colonial officers, folklorists and the missionaries to study and understand local traditions and cultures. They published essays and articles in the magazines and journals of Asiatic Society as well as books to make us Indians aware of our indigenous traditions. Such activities were, to a large extent, responsible for the development of a nationalist consciousness among the people of India. Even Rabindranath Tagore took to writing about Bengali *gaan, brata* etc.

The Odia literary community is dominated by poets, who brought about an awareness of folk literature, thus encouraging research in the field. Folk culture, however, has had to wait. The author of this book has taken up for investigation home-bred treasures: songs of the heart, set to country music. Those days Abanindra Tagore's Bengali book on *brata* set the pace for research on folk culture in India. Later, several scholars went on to write books on folk culture based on research; Kapila Vatsyayan's *Traditional Indian Theatre: Multiple Streams* is an example. Odia researchers of folk culture include Dhiren Das, Bhabagrahi Mishra, Arabinda Pattanaik, Mahendra Mishra and Anjali Padhi. Bhagyalipi Malla is the newest addition to this list. She deserves credit for this exercise.

'Know thyself' is the purport of what the author has set out to do, and, hence, this book is firmly implanted in Odia consciousness. As Rabindaranth Tagore says in *Atma Parichay*, "Whoever abandons his own, will never be able to make others his own. If you do not accept your own land and people, you must not expect others to take cognisance of you." Our pride and self-respect depends on our awareness and knowledge of Odia culture. Whether this author's exercise is appreciated will, of course, depend on the sense of responsibility and self-esteem among readers and the choices they make.

The history of self-knowledge among Odias goes back only to the later part of nineteenth century. It was because of the British colonial rule and the western influence as well as the cultural and political domination of non-Odias, especially the Bengalis, that there occurred an awakening of Odia nationalist consciousness, and Odia language gained status as the official language of the state. All those who acknowledged Odia as their mother tongue were considered as of the Odia race.

More than a millennium ago, the whole of the Indian

subcontinent was guided by an all-encompassing ideal of Indian culture. Around the seventh or eighth century, with political alignments and re-alignments, feudatory rulers rose to prominence which resulted in consolidation of regional cultural aspirations. Regional languages and literatures flourished in Assam, Bengal, Bihar and Odisha which, probably, were once part of a common cultural and linguistic area. These acquired distinctive identities and became separate political units. For example, the "Charyapada" might have been written at a time when Ahomiya, Bengali, Maithili and Odia were present in their ancient *abahatta* form. The prakrit form of Sanskrit took shape in these regions. The prakrits, at a later stage, might have acquired local flavours to give birth to Bengali, Odia and Assamese languages, each with its own system of writing. It was thus that a particular stream from among the Indo-Aryan languages came to known as Odia.

Modern Odia used to be called variously as prakrit bhasha or Utkaliya bhasha. It is not known with certainty how the name Odia came to be used for this language. As a distinct race, Odias were known from antiquity. Perhaps the language was first called Odia and then all those who spoke the language came to be known as Odias. The rise of language-based identities was a nineteenth century phenomenon. Of course, Odia identity derives justification from what is generally understood as Indian identity.

The central concepts of Indian thought such as *brahm*, *karma* and belief in death and reincarnation are essential components of Odia culture too. It is true we have our distinct and exclusive cultural icons such as Ta'poi but it is the pan-Indian figures such as Lakshmi, Sita and Savitri who dominate our cultural consciousness. However, to avoid being subsumed by an overarching Indian identity, we need to be deeply aware of our own regional culture and identity. Those of us who take no pride in our land's culture would eventually find no ground to stand on.

Odia culture is not only thousands of years old but also has diversified into numerous branches representing traditions new and old, upheavals and new evolving ideals of life and living. The ancient 'samaj' of Ashoka's inscriptions, for example, traversed through centuries of change to stand transformed as modern-day '*phula jatra*'. According to the famous cultural anthropologist Robert Redfield, culture finds expression at two levels: the 'great tradition' and the 'little tradition'. The former takes shape in urban institutions while the latter grows and develops in the countryside. The great poet Yeats has said that all beautiful things in this world are created by three categories of people: the nobility lays down the customs and norms of behaviour, the country folk gives us our myths and stories, the artists create the rest. All those ingredients which comprise the Odia world-view form such a long list that one would be in want of a deep abiding interest to know them all. Bhagyalipi, therefore, has taken great care to focus on only the extant popular and communal forms of art and culture, which were born out of the needs and aspirations of rural agricultural communities. Naturally, these forms are fast undergoing change; still, the author has tried her best to capture the contemporaneity of these expressions. For this, she has travelled the length and breadth of the state to understand the distinctive cultural traits of various regions. No Indian, or Odia, for that matter, is unaware of *Rama lila* or *rasa lila*. But the *Rama lila* of Odisha is certainly different from *ram lila* elsewhere — this is what the author has tried to show through her depiction of various performances, all experienced personally and uniquely.

The aim of the author is not to explain the origins of or historicise the performance traditions but to provide an intimate experience so as to inspire an empathic appreciation of one's own culture. She has been largely successful in this regard. I congratulate her for this second successful enterprise after *Kala Kalantar*, which was published in 2016, and thank her for choosing me to introduce her collection. I wish Bhagyalipi all the very best.

Dasharathi Das

Author's Note

From Matthew Arnold to Arjun Appadurai, one sees no end to debates about culture. According to them, it is culture which moulds man. In other words, all that man needs to live and thrive constitutes 'culture'. Culture and civilisation always go together. What we call civilisation is a particular moment in the history of time, a representation of the composite nature of the products of man's creative faculties. A civilisation, therefore, never dies and continues to live on through culture, reflecting the progress of time. It is in this cultural flow that a human being and his beliefs, philosophy and creative outlook keep changing.

If someone were to ask me about my culture, I would present myself for the purpose. At the same time it has to be said that I carry within myself the traits of several empathic known and as-yet-unknown selves who keep changing with time. My culture and I, thus, carry the stamp of the eternal and the universal. 'The five great elements' which sustain us, are the gifts from God, which form the essential ingredients of our material culture. To understand the world around us as well as to give it a meaning, we create our own philosophies as well as different forms of art and religion all of which comprise our culture. But who could have given human beings the secret to create, mould and give shape? Man, thus, is not just made in the likeness of God the creator, but is the creator himself.

Who created culture? This question is often asked. Sometimes, it is created by an individual and it gets accepted and appreciated by the community; sometimes it is created by a group of people while sometimes it is created by the desire of those in power. When these creations enter and influence the life flow of a community, it becomes culture. But, as it is driven by the force of the spirit, all creation, including the purely material, is spiritual in nature.

Since the time of birth of consciousness, Nature and her workings have preoccupied human thought and attention and the mysterious benign and malignant forces of Nature have begun to be represented, variously, as gods and goddesses and demons and devils. It became necessary for these forces to be appeased or controlled and this gave rise to the worship of stones and trees and the moon and the sun. Gradually, the human desire for beauty and perfection gave birth to magnificent stone carvings and houses for the gods, and wondrous abstract forms of expression in the form of rituals and norms to guide and celebrate life and living. In this book, I have focused on the typically Odia forms of such expression. In doing so, I hope I have brought home to the readers an awareness of the distinctiveness of Odia culture as also an understanding of the connectedness of the Odia tradition with the cultures of the wider world around us.

My sincere thanks to the leading Odia daily *The Prameya* and it's Editor Mr. Gopal Krishna Mohapatra for publishing this book in the form of a feature article, every fortnight for many years. This helped me to reach out a wider readership and earned me reader's love and appreciation.

Bhagyalipi Malla
Odisha State Museum

Translator's note

Books like *Asmitara Abhilekha*, whenever they come, serve one important purpose: to draw attention to the excessively parsimonious use in India of scholarly acumen to study folk culture. In her article titled "India on the Map of 'Hard Science' Folkloristics", written in 1983 for the journal *Folklore*, Heda Jason explains how India woke up to folk culture only after gaining independence. "The rising Indian modern national consciousness had no need to seek support by reference to its folk culture. Like the Greek and Jewish national movements, the Indian movement could build on its extremely rich national classical heritage, featuring great works in all arts and humanities, a basis which the young, just awakening European nations could not boast of." In contrast, the Chinese struggle for nation-state building during the early decades of twentieth century was largely sustained by a movement 'from below', when a group of teachers at National Beijing University started looking for vernacular works in folk culture "to support the Literary Revolution which advocated replacing classical Chinese with vernacular language in literature. It was under these circumstances that modern folklore study originated in early twentieth century China" (Jie Gao, "Saving the Nation Through Culture: The Folklore Movement in Republican China (1918-1949)", Ph. D. thesis, U. of Western Ontario).

In India, folklore scholarship began as a mainly colonial enterprise in the last quarter of the nineteenth century; it was primarily the British officers and the women who took note of folklore. It is somewhat known that a large number of educated Indians were involved as 'native informants' in the collection and transcription of folktales. However, we know very little about these Indian collectors, mainly because the colonial officers did not care to acknowledge the labours of the 'native informants'. This is borne out by Sadhana Naithani's illuminating account of the tensions, caused by imbalance of power, between the British colonial officer William Crooke and his punctilious Indian 'assistant' Pandit Ram Gharib Chaube, who translated hundreds of north Indian folktales into English for Crooke's project. Chaube is said to have lost his mind in the later years of his life, due, in no small measure, to the "deathly anonymity" that had been imposed upon him in the colonial enterprise. As far as the conceptualisation of the identity of such Indian collectors is concerned, Naithani's book *In Quest of Indian Folktales: Pandit Ram Gharib Chaube and William Crooke* is a classic postcolonial archive.

Bhagyalipi Malla's *Asmitara Abhilekha* is about Odia folk culture, an ensemble of Odia cultural expressions, which makes my position as a translator of *Asmitara Abhilekha* somewhat different from that of Pandit Chaube. As an Indian, I have inherited a historical experience of colonialism and hence am aware of the contingencies of translating for a western English reader but the colonial experience is not the most significant of my experiences as an individual. This means, my concern is less to create a context such that the profundity of a particular act or ritual is made clear and more to not be considered as unrepresentative of my people and to be considered as one among many legitimate spokespersons of Odia culture. If one finds blind lists for, say, the musical instruments used for a particular performance, I have only one thing to say: There are things only those who live / have lived in Odisha understand. The author and I, who are both witnesses of and actors in these performances, are equal collaborators, and thus, I claim no victimhood but the right to celebrate.

For some Odia words, as those used for the musical instruments for example, I have used romanised transcription. Odia readers can easily decipher the word from the simplified transcription, while others need not worry about the exact pronunciation of the Odia words.

Urmishree Bedamatta
Asst. Professor, Department of English,
Ravenshaw University, Odisha

Reviewer's note

Odia culture is one of the most vibrant cultures in India and its rural culture forms its backbone. Rural areas of Odisha have got a simple culture transmitted from generation to generation. Bhagyalipi's *Asmitara Abhilekha: Ama Sanskrutira Gatha* is a book on different aspects of the culture of rural Odisha. It encompasses forty-five aspects of this culture that includes different *oshas*, *bratas*, pala, dance, songs, musical instruments, *rasalila*, festivals, dramatic representations, *jatras*, etc. All these constitute a unique record of the identity of the Odias. Once upon a time such things were ubiquitous but these days they are treated as trivial, insignificant and ludicrous. But as we know, folk culture is gradually gaining prominence and in this regard Bhagyalipi's work is significant. Although she has not dealt with folk music and folk stories, the different *oshas*, *bratas*, dance forms and dramatic representations she has written about are, in fact, a precious treasure of Odia society.

Authors such as Dhiren Das, Bhagirathi Mishra, Arabinda Patnaik, Mahendra Mishra and Anjali Padhi have written about folk culture. Bhagyalipi's book is a new addition to the field. She has tried to improve upon the already existing of writing about Odia folk culture with her individual talent. This book gives full vent to her feelings of patriotism, sub-nationalism and love for Odisha. Narrating the different aspects of Odia rural culture, she has given stress on Odia cultural identity. In fact, the rural people of Odisha have played a very important role in building Odia culture. The famous 'Jagannath dharma' is basically a folk religion which forms a part of Odia culture.

Her book lays emphasis on the traditional socio-religious culture of Odisha which encompasses different social customs, rites and rituals such as marriages and *brata*s or religious observances, pujas and worships (Durga Puja, Ramalila, Dolayatra) *osha*s and fasts (religious observances and fasting) of girls and women, several festivals based on social and religious life of Odia people, the paika and chhau dance forms, dramatic performances, songs, etc. Bhagyalipi has confined herself to discussions of such aspects of Odia culture that provide joy both at the domestic and social levels. She has depicted a miniscule but significant part of rural Odia culture which was built by villagers because life was village-centric in the past. The festivals, *jatra*s, *osha*s, *brata*s and fasts of Odisha are diverse and many. The writer has selected only a few. But she has given adequate attention to each of these selected aspects and discussed each one elaborately.

Now life has gone away from the hands of artists and fallen into the hands of traders and skilled workers. Culture is being separated from rural heritage and life is devoid of joy which rural heritage once provided the people. The visual art forms of villages are gradually becoming obsolete. Bhagyalipi has held on to the folk culture of the past and written this book. Her effort is laudable. From this book we come to know about the richness of Odia culture of the villages of Odisha.

Her essays included in the book show her erudition, understanding, imagination and insight. She has investigated the history, tradition and evolution of various aspects of Odia rural culture. While doing so she has taken the help of smrutis, puranas, anthropology, sociology, journalism and her own experiences as well as her imagination. While discussing "Tika Gobindachandra", "Lalita Pala" or "Chakulia Panda", she has approached the topics with a researcher's mind. In fact, all her writings are scholarly, full of facts, attractive, logical and research-oriented. She has united her emotion and imagination with her poetic and analytical mind to make her essays fascinating so much so that the *osha*s, *brata*s and *lila*s described and analysed by her become very much interesting to the readers.

The purpose of the writer is to intimately acquaint the readers with the rural culture of Odisha. She has thought it as her national responsibility to bring this culture to the public at large. She has willingly taken this duty upon herself.

Nowadays, identity matters much. In order to know the Odias, one must know their culture. In India, there are several states and regions having different cultures. But people having one culture know almost nothing about other cultures. Unity in our country cannot be brought by state power. It can be achieved by knowing, understanding and intermingling of different cultures of the country. When cultural exchanges take place, and we know about the best traditions of others, we can develop a loving relationship with them. We may have a provincial identity but we should have a pan-Indian identity as well as a human identity. Real humanity lies in human solidarity, harmony and unity in diversity. Every province, country or race may have great variety. This should not lead to exclusivity and separation. Unity in diversity is a precious thing. But a sense of identity is a significant element in strengthening the relationship with others. So provincial or regional identity is welcome. But there should be interaction among various cultures.

In India, we should encourage cultural exchanges between one state and another. This will lead to better understanding and relationship. Here, translation of different works would help. By translating Bhagyalipi's book into English Urmishree has done a commendable job. Whereas the original text has forty-seven aspects of the rural culture of Odisha, Urmishree has merged some aspects and pruned some essays where she felt it was necessary. This English translation will certainly help the non-native readers who are interested in Odia culture. A regional culture will have scope to be introduced to the more powerful national culture of India. Moreover, the translation will be made available to a readership outside our country.

Urmishree's translation is a faithful translation but it is not a word-by-word translation. She has, undoubtedly, preserved the original matter and form of the essays. The rendering has been done without sacrificing the source text by making a compromise between the language and thought of the work translated by the language and thought of the new medium. There is utter fidelity to the sense of the original work. The translator has been much concerned with the words of the author and the spirit of the source text. Semantic correspondence has engaged the attention of the translator. However, she has 'condensed, distilled and sublimated' the original essays wherever she felt it was necessary.

Bijaya Kumar Nanda

CONTENTS

The worship of Shakti　25

The secret of *Rasa*　29

Lakshmi Purana and the worship of Lakshmi　39

Deities, *osha* and the Odia household　45

Journey with no end: Bargarh Dhanujatra　57

Ramalila　61

O Mountains, O Trees…How is my Lord　67

The lost world of puppets　73

The goddesses of Odisha and the rural carnival　77

Danda nata　79

Pala: May there be no suffering, 'Hari Hari Bol'　83

Sabitri brata: A story of love, death and immortality　87

Lalita *pala*　90

Raja parba: Let the mind soar	93
Dasakathia: 'Chant the holy name of Rama'	97
Mogul Tamsa: Beware! Here comes Mirza sahib!	103
The dear little sister who craved for a few broken grains of paddy	107
Chhau dance	111
'Sabda nrutya': Nada and its expressions	115
Dalkhai: An intimate experience of Shakti	119
The snake charmer and a song for his snake	125
Dancing for the Lord: Sakhi nata, Gotipua, and the devadasi	129
Makar sankranti, *Pusha punei*, and bond of friendship	133
Ghumura and Paika: Of battle sounds and war dance	139
Ghoda nata: Hey you town-bred man! Tell me how many breeds of horses there are...	145
Tika Gobindachandra: Do you or not chant the holy name of Rama?	149
Chakulia Panda: As you give, so shall you receive...	155
The call of the wild: Tiger dance	159
Go slow, O palanquin bearers: The Odia song of Lament	163
Banajaga and the story of Nabakalebar	169
Bibliography	174

The worship of Shakti

What could be the reason behind Kali's frightful form and fierce nature? The demon Mahishasura was arrogant and haughty, and disrespectful to his elders, parents and the sages. His actions made Mother Earth tremble in terror and he made eyes at women. The devas, unable to slay him, were forced to seek the protection of Shakti. They bequeathed upon her their weapons and might: Agni gave her the three eyes, Yama her hair, Himalaya gave her a lion to ride on, Indra gave her Airavat, Brahma gave her the rosary, Surya gave her his energy and Vishnu his discus. Bedecked in Nature's elemental splendour, Shakti now proceeds to fight with her son. Faced with her son's arrogance, the Mother feels helpless and embarks on a lila of annihilation. She roars, "It is me that you are lusting for! Look at me. I dare you!" and appears before him in full nakedness. Poor Mahishasura, unable to bear the splendour of the cosmic spiritual source, is paralysed, and exterminated.

It is true the Mother slayed her son. But unable to bear the shock, she rages on and destroys everybody who comes her way. The devas cry in fear and seek the refuge of Shakti's beloved husband Shiva. Shiva instantly brings from heaven Shakti's beloved Parijata flower and holds it up for her while lying down on her way. Shakti hurries to hold the flower and treads upon her husband. Realising her folly, Shakti calms down and becomes conscious of what she is doing. Her followers and attendants, wherever they are, stand still. It is in this state of benign calmness that they continue to be worshipped as *gramadevati* in every village in Utkal today. In the different seats of worship, she is worshipped as Mahakali.

Woman is the symbol of Shakti, the life-giving force. Shakti is the reason of birth, death, life and progress. Shakti is the reason, too, of creation based on the scientific premise, big bang. All that took place during and after the big bang was an image of Shakti in multifarious forms. It is thus that Shakti is considered as the primal cause of all things. Man is only a medium through which Shakti operates. The life cycle and the creative energy of man is controlled by none other than Shakti. It is why man devoid of energy is lifeless. Shakti is at the root of all creative expressions: kavya, purana, stotra and architecture, art and music. Aurobindo has discussed the three forms of Shakti, namely, Mahalakshmi, Mahasaraswati and Mahakali. Thus, Shakti is the goddess of birth, progress and liberation. Therefore, She is all-pervading and She manifests herself in wonderful and variegated forms.

When we worship the Mother, we tell her, we are of you. Unable to fathom your love, beauty and sacrifice, we become blind with arrogance and pride. We beg you to release us from self-pride. You are the cause of all creation. Here lies beneath your feet your beloved who knows how well you love the Parijata, the symbol of your love, kindness, simplicity and innocence.

Man is fully aware of a woman's weakness. If he didn't know

her weakness, he wouldn't have been able to control her. It is for this reason that Shiva held out the Parijata for Shakti, who on beholding the flower was reminded of her original benign self and the world was saved. Shakti, in her benign avatar, becomes Adimata and blesses one and all. It is this form of Shakti that human beings have forever revered and worshipped.

In Odia homes, Durga is worshipped in the form of idols made of mud, stone, bell-metal or bronze. Shakti was the most-worshipped deity in ancient Odisha, famously known as "Uddiyan peeth", when several temples sprang up for the worship of goddess in all her forms. The temples include: Mohini, Kapalini and Gouri temples in Bhubaneswar; Harchandi and Bimala in Puri; Kichakeswari in Khiching; Biraja in Jajpur; Mangala in Kakatpur; Charchika in Banki; Barahi in Chaurashi; Sarala in Jhankada; Samaleswari in Sambalpur; Saptamatruka in Puri and Jajpur; and Chausathi jogini in Hirapur and Ranipur, Jharial. One finds invocations to Shakti in several early literary works such as Sarala Das's *Mahabharata* and *Chandi Purana*, Balaram Das's *Lakshmi Purana* and *Bata Abakasha*, Dwarka Das's *Manasa mangala* written in Odia mixed with Bengali, Shitalicharan's *Dwarika pala*, *Durga rahasya* of Madhusudan Harichandan, *Chandi charitamrita* of Ajambar Singh and *Ambika vilasa* of Brajanath Badajena.

The secret of *Rasa*

It is the end of the season of *Sharad*. And winter is waiting at the door. The clear sky and the effulgent natural surroundings bring peace and calm to one's soul. It is when one can almost see Mahayogi deeply contemplating the beautiful and radiant face of Mahamaya. There occurs a surge of desire for creation in both; Mahamaya and Mahayogi are transformed into Radha and Krishna, and the stage is set for Maharasa. One feels and experiences the beauty of the union and calls it *rasa lila* or *sharad râsa*. To celebrate the experience, the human mind conceptualises *kartika purnima* as *rasa purnima*. On this occasion, Brajbhumi of Vrindavan becomes the centre of Radha and Krishna's *râsa*. The lila of Radha and Krishna is celebrated once in two months. Of these lila, it is *sharad* and *vasant râsa* which are much awaited and celebrated.

On a *rasa purnima* evening, the whole village gathers to witness Krishna's *gopa lila*. At the centre of a bedecked stage are Radha and Krishna circled by gopis. They dance to drumbeats and their movements are filled with shringar rasa. Sometimes, they play love-games; at other times, they quarrel, and, their gestures are expressive of the magnificence of creation. Is this what holds the audience spellbound?

Who are Krishna, Radha, the gopis, and where are these places -- Mathura, Gopa, Brindavan, Dwarka situated? Over time, these characters and places have acquired various meanings in our cultural expressions such as religion, philosophy, literature, art, architecture, dance, drama and music. It is said these characters, the independent male and female elements were born out of human consciousness, and that the union of these elements is the cause of all creation, of past present and future. But who is Krishna? Krishna is a worthy man; He is unique among men. He has unparalleled attractiveness, qualities and valour. He is mighty and powerful yet forgiving. He is an enchanter but also a real human being. He has form yet is beyond form; He can be heard but is beyond hearing; He can be perceived, yet is inexpressible. He is supreme ego, yet is in a state of complete surrender. He is a mix of opposites, hence, is mysterious. Krishna is the independent self-sufficient *purusha*; the gopis are *prakriti*, dependent on and attached to Krishna. Krishna combines in himself the best of all males. Therefore, it is but natural that all the rest surrender to him. Who are they that surrender? They are *prakriti*, the women. To entice Krishna and capture his attention they adopt all the strategies of seduction such as, attiring and adorning, dance, song, music, acting and indulge in all kinds of playful emotional banter. It is the desire for creation that draws these women to the supreme *purusha*, Krishna. The drama of emotions that results from this desire is known as *râsa*.

Is it possible that many surrender to one and only one? This question has led to the birth of philosophy. Philosophers have tried to explain this in various ways: some say, that the human being is controlled by ego and guided by the desires of the self. An ego-driven human being achieves a state of surrender only through the annihilation of ego. The reason for surrender is enchantment, not fear and one derives ultimate pleasure from complete surrender. The *Bhagavat Purana* explains the essence of such surrender in chapters 28 to 33 comprising the *rasapanchadhyayi* section of tenth canto. The setting of *râsapanchadhyayi* is the season of *sharad* when prakriti and purusha are filled with the desire for creation and the desire for union is there in their mind. The place is Brindavan on the banks of Yamuna on a full moon night. The sound of the flute is heard through the souls. The gopis have left behind all worldly attachments and, each gopi, with a Krishna for herself, dances away the night. Such is the time when one's consciousness is filled with a subtle awareness of the union.

However, there occurs a rupture in the gopis' experience

Rasamandal

when they are filled with self-pride for having attained Krishna. They start looking upon Krishna as a human being and try to have Him all for themselves. Krishna soon disappears from the scene and the gopis wail. Soon they lose individual identity and thus become free from fear and stop wailing. They are so engrossed in thoughts of Krishna that they override their sense of separateness and separation from Krishna. Krishna returns to them later after having taught the gopis a lesson in selfless love. All this is but an imaginative representation of spiritual love. Philosophers have tried to explain the possibility of ego-less self. It is not easy to attain it, they say, but it is possible. They have envisioned Radha as emblematic of such a self. The figure of Radha itself has been a subject of much conjecture. Radha does not figure in the Bhagavata but the purana mentions 'anayoradhika', meaning a worshipper. It is said, Radhika appeared in South India in the eighth century. From there she came to Odisha.

However, it is Jayadeva's *Gitagovinda* which gives full expression to the figure of Radha, one who is in love with and in state of complete devotion and surrender to Krishna. Radha is the subtle form of the gopi who is completely devoted to Krishna. Poets, however, have transformed Radha and Krishna into human beings, who are troubled by the usual cares, concerns and conflicts of the world. But in the twelfth century Jayadeva, in his Gitagovinda, has depicted Radha as one who is enchanted by Krishna and has colpletely surrendered to Him. Thus he has laid emphasis on complete surrender in love. To propagate this philosophy, Jayadeva's poem has been brought to Jagannath temple as a play to be performed during the *badasinghar* [sleep] ritual of the Lord. Jagannath has been visualised as the joint representation of Radha and Krishna. Several saints such as Madhva, Nimbarka, Vallabhacharya and Chaitanya have upheld and propagated the idea of Radha and Krishna as an eternal pair and experienced the ecstasy of divine love. This love has led to the establishment of a casteless and classless social order in which people are held together by nothing but love. This led a body blow to Brahminism and even the king Prataprudra Dev walked the path of *prema bhakti*.

In *rasa lila*, Krishna is known as the human form of *Brahm*. Through his activities, he shows how the roles that a human being performs in life are real. It is when one becomes self-centred that one is filled with fear and anxiety. A relationship based on unconditional love and devoid of egotism alone fills one with bliss, and hence is spiritual love.

Why is Gopapura at the centre of *rasa lila*? Krishna lived in Mathura and Dwarka too. In Dwarka Krishna is *tamas*: is a king and has many wives; in Mathura he is a power-wielder and a devoted lover and has the qualities of *rajas* and *tamas;* in Gopapura he is a child who fascinates with his pranks and overwhelms with undiluted love and concern for all. Knowledge

Rasalila in Pattachitra

Rasalila in Bhitichitra

of Self is the only true knowledge and is forever worthy of attainment yet it cannot be attained without paying attention to the body and its cares, as is explained by "*rasapanchadhyayi*". Krishna's flute plays on the desires of the mind and body causing the gopis to abandon home and hearth and rush to Him. The call of the supreme *rasika* endures as the gopis shed their inhibitions and ego to surrender with love and devotion and the *lila* continues. A crucial part of *lila* is the elegant circular dance in which every gopi has a Krishna for herself; this dance is the main attraction of *Vasanta Rasa* [springtime *lila*]. It is not known for certain when and how Radha Krishna lila came to be associated with the spring season. However, that *vasanta rasa* has ancient roots is found in the compositions of Shatanand Acharya of eleventh century (see the collection titled *Shatanand Sangraha*). The scene and setting of *vasanta rasa* as is described in *rasapanchadhyayi* of *Bhagavata Purana* finds an exquisite representation in Jayadeva's *Gita Govinda* (12th c.). It is this *vasanta rasa* again which finds distinctive expression, later, in the

Rasalila: A Madhubani painting

compositions of Bidyapati, Ramananda Pattanayak, Krushnadas and Chandidas.

Bondi nata

While Radha Krishna *lila* continues to be a popular art form in Odisha, *Bondi nata,* a popular performance in the mountainous regions of Odisha, brings into perspective a lesser-known episode in the tradition of Radha Krishna *lila*. It is about Bondi, the Odia name for Kutila who is the sister of Chandrasena, the husband of Radha. Bondi, unable to tolerate the accusations of impotence against her brother, accuses Radha of adultery and shamelessness. Her act, which is made up of sexually explicit dialogues and gestures, not only provides great entertainment to the people who keep asking for more but also is a powerful

raging critique against human sexual urge which leads quite a few on the path to depravity and sinfulness.

Laudi [cowherd's staff] khela

The story of Radha and Krishna is the subject of yet another folk performance called *laudi khela*. In the month of Phagun which is the beginning of spring season, the gopalas [cowherd community] of Odisha, sing the *Gopala ogala*, narrating the frolics of the young Krishna: In Phagun, He is Gobinda who plays with colours / He mixes fire from the arms factory with the colours / And continues to play. The gopalas walk through the village streets, singing and dancing, while hitting their staff on the ground as if to give a call to the young maidens who are inside the house to come out and have fun. They perform mock fights with their sticks which are moved and turned so fast that they become invisible. On *panchu dola*, the tenth day of the bright fortnight of Phagun, the gopalas walk in a procession amid drum beats and the sound of cymbals and mahuri, as they carry around the image or idol of baby Krishna in a small wooden temple. Krishna visits every home where He is worshipped by the family members and a handful of colours is exchanged between the gopalas and the family.

The gopalas are dressed in white and wear colourful turbans, waistbands, and flower garlands. Their faces are decorated with sandalwood paste and vermilion. *Gopala ogala* songs, which are sung in the form of dialogues, comprise sixteen lilas such as *bastra harana, kaliya dalana, Indra bibada, Garuda-Hanu kalaha, sarpabhisara, banshi chori* etc. The enactment of nine philosophies of life such as *singha benu rahasya, Gayatri tattva, chita tattva* and *guhala tattva*, etc. and, stories about daily life in cowherd communities such as grazing the cattle, milking of cows, selling of milk and curd etc. Gopapura is at the centre of all performances.

The composition called *Gopala ogala* is said to have been composed by the great saint Achyutananda of Tilakana village. Born of Dinabandhu and Padmabati, Achyutananda was an ardent devotee of Krishna. He is also the author of two well-known Odia texts, *Harivamsa* and *Shunya samhita*. It is not known for sure what motivated Achyutananda to write a composition like *Gopala ogala*. It may very well have been written as a reaction against the elitist attitudes of Brahmins towards members of lower castes. In the olden days, the gopalas or the yadavas were considered as one among thirty-six sub-clans of the royal clan of Rajputs. The gopalas consider themselves as chandravanshi [those who worship the moon as the god of the clan] and of Krishna gotra. They were a valorous race and extremely well-trained in the wielding of weapons.

Gajalakshmi: Raja Ravi Varma's Oleograph

Lakshmi Purana and the worship of Lakshmi

In Margashira, the most auspicious month of the year, one begins to savour the exquisite flavours of Nature when among green shrubby ripples, half-ripe rice crops proudly wave their golden panicles which are constantly bent in embarrassment. The grain-yards are laden with sheaves of harvested paddy and the stakes of threshing floors stand strong and erect, village walls are flushed with red earth and blaze with floral designs made with the watery paste of sunned rice. Among the designs are the endearingly small lotus feet of Lakshmi.

In Odisha, every Thursday of Margashira is dedicated to the worship of the beautiful and benign Lakshmi. On this day, she, whose throne is the lotus, and who is the consort of Vishnu, prepares to visit her fellow women and queens of the households after making customary rounds of fields and grain-yards. Lakshmi is the goddess of dutifulness and good grace and gives close attention to details of behaviour and thought.

A single misstep could earn her wrath and drive her away. Nothing could be worse.

The lady of the house, with great imagination and care, tries to give form to her vision of the ethereal and sublime Lakshmi. For this, she draws fine designs with rice paste on the walls of the granary. On a small wooden stool she seats a corn-measuring bamboo vessel (mana) overflowing with newly harvested rice (the mana itself is cleaned with clarified butter, fragrant oil and turmeric and on it are designs drawn with rice paste), the thick paddy tassels hanging down. She then gives shape to the eyes and nose with sandalwood and turmeric paste and finally applies a resplendent dot of red vermilion on the mana and veils it with a red printed cloth and colourful flowers. A ceremonial jar filled with water is carefully set in front of the image. Through the image of Lakshmi created with great love and care, the lady of the house, with deep devotion, invokes the bounteous spirit of Laskhmi, amid wafts of perfumed resin. For offerings, there are several kinds of boiled and fried rice cakes and an assortment of fruits including coconut and sugarcane attractively laid out in a plate. In this holy communion of Lakshmi and her devotee, a fellow woman, there is no role for the man. It is the lady of the house who, after finishing the worship rituals, ties the turmeric-laced sacred thread with ten knots on her arm. Each knot is for the ten blessings which she has sought from the divine mother for her family.

The worship of the bountiful and graceful feminine spirit which Lakshmi embodies is not a practice among only the Odias of India. The maypole dance of European countries, too, celebrates such a spirit. The Greek pantheon has Demeter, the goddess of agriculture.

In ancient Indian agricultural society, Lakshmi was not worshipped in homes. She was worshipped by the village commune which deposited its harvest in the village grain-yard.

The communal worship of Lakshmi must have helped keep the community together. Gradually, with the rise of farmers with independent land holdings, Lakshmi began to be worshipped in individual homes.

Lakshmi appears as Sri in Srisukta of Rig Veda. She again makes an appearance in the Mahabharata in the episode of the churning of the Ocean of Milk. Among several things that emanate as a result of the churning is Sri or Lakshmi. She is Mother Nature herself. Furthermore, she appears as the wife of Vishnu in various incarnations—as Rama's wife Sita, Krishna's wife Rukmini and Nrusingha's wife Lakshmi. In architecture and paintings, Lakshmi has four hands. The two right hands exhibit gestures of assurance (*abhaya mudra*) and compassion (*varada mudra*) and the left hands hold up a conch and the sun. Her vehicle is the owl. In the Jagannath Temple at Puri, Lakshmi is worshipped in two forms, Sridevi and Bhudevi. Ramanuja, who visited Puri in the twelfth century, rechristened the land as Srikshetra and the temple as Srimandir. Sri Aurobindo, in Durga stotra, emphasises the need for a

A bronze idol of Lakshmi

Lakshmi in Pattachitra

righteous approach to wealth. Gandhiji's idea of trusteeship is based on this ideal. Gandhi explains how illegal production, selfish enjoyment and hoarding leads to all-round degradation and despair. With the passage of time, the image of Lakshmi has undergone a change. She is no more the bounteous and free-giving mother. She has been transformed into the goddess of wealth. She no more holds crops in her hands but is seen giving away golden coins.

Sri occupies a significant place in the Odia imagination, as is exemplified by Balarama Das's *Lakshmi Purana*. While Balarama highlights Lakshmi as wife and mother, the 17th century *Nrusingha Purana* by Pitambara Dasa highlights the amorous relationship between Lakshmi and Nrusingha. Lakshmi is also known as Chanchala, one who does not reside in a place for a long time. Any slight in behaviour and morals would make her leave and usher in the reign of sorrow.

Balarama Das's *Lakshmi Purana* has been immensely popular in Odisha and is the subject of numerous scholarly debates about the author and the original form and metre of the text. The narrative is about Sri, who, while doing her customary rounds of the town, finds dirt lying around everywhere. When she reaches the Chandala (untouchable caste) hamlet, she is impressed by Shriya, who has taken every care to keep her surroundings clean and worship Lakshmi with utmost devotion. Lakshmi enters her house and blesses her. Balarama comes to know of Lakshmi's adventure. Balarama, with his deeply ingrained caste values, is enraged and forces his younger brother Jagannath to throw Lakshmi out of the temple. With her self-pride hurt, Lakshmi leaves and settles in a palace of her own by the sea. After numerous travails, Balarama realises that Lakshmi had done no wrong.

Scholars tend to see *Lakshmi Purana* as an avant-garde text in that it questions the deeply entrenched values which support social discrimination and exploitation. However, the love between Jagannath and Lakshmi is no less important. Jagannath is a true friend when he tells Lakshmi that if he had seen her in the *chandaluni*'s house, he would have never spoken about it. Like a true householder, Jagannath suffers immensely in Lakshmi's separation even as he remains by the side of his elder brother. When Lakshmi, at the doorstep, hears her Lord chanting the Vedas, the goddess and wife cries in despair for having caused trouble to her husband by deserting him and abandons her anger to take her place in the temple as Shakti incarnate when Jagannath, at Balarama's behest, invites her to go there. For every Odia, therefore, *Lakshmi Purana* embodies the sacredness of family life, love and responsibilities.

I offer my prayers, O Mother Kamala

Jhoti

Lakshmi Mandala

Deities, *osha* and the Odia household

The average Odia woman has a deity to worship and a ritual to perform almost every day in a year. On some days there are two separate pujas to be performed and the surroundings resonate with the sound of the conch, the drum beats and joyful trilling. Whether it is a girl attaining puberty or there is someone who has fallen sick or there occurs a pleasant event, there are deities to take care of every event and every occasion, good and bad. Indeed, every Odia believes that there are thirty-three crore deities in all. Like human beings, these gods have homes and families. However, unlike human beings they do not die. Odisha, being home to the Lord of the Universe, Jagannath, it is but natural that all the gods have made this land their home, and hence is called *deva bhoomi* [the land of the gods].

However, not all deities are remembered and worshipped with equal importance. Of late, several new deities such as Santoshi and Gojabayani have taken birth and some older deities have nearly been forgotten. Prior to them, we had several ritual fasts such as *budhei osha, khudurukuni osha, shathi osha, sukutuni osha, bhai jiuntia osha, pausha rabibara osha, kartika somabara osha, chaiti mangalabara osha*, etc. There are several other ritual fasts performed in every nook and corner of this region and are yet to be listed. We even have a name for a woman performing such fasts, "Osheiti". Women fast and conduct rituals not only to please the good gods but also to appease the bad and ugly gods such as Bâdi Thakurani. Their ululations, it is said, drive the bad gods out.

The Odia word 'osha', which means ritual fasting, is believed to have been derived either from the Sanskrit 'uposhana' or the Pali 'upabasatha'. To perform osha, one is expected to follow a set of ten rules: purity, forgiveness, kindness, charity, personal cleanliness, abstinence from sensual pleasures, worshipping of the gods, fire worship, contentment, and non-covetousness. Osha is mainly a female-dominated domain and the deities worshipped for osha are of this world.

In comparison with others, Odias are more empathic and are of accepting nature. For this reason, they may be considered either courageous or fearful. Whatever it may be, Odias are multicultural and hold diverse beliefs. From the mountains to the sea, every community and every region has a deity of its own. Belief in the deity's powers offers solace to the human being who finds it impossible to logically explain the presence of varied kinds of beings on this earth and the occurrence of various natural phenomena. To worship the deities, they choose different settings: at the foot of the mountain or mountain top, beside a tree, a riverbank, by the side of the pond or a stream or on the sea beach; for some others a place is made in front of one's own house, in the courtyard or backyard, on the street, the village ending or inside a temple. The deities come in various forms, shapes and sizes: some look fearsome and forbidding, some have red eyes, some have blood dripping from their mouth, some are enchantingly beautiful, some have a bewitching smile, some are calm, some are wrathful, some are fully-dressed and bedecked with all sorts of ornaments, some are half-naked or naked; some are proficient in the nine arts; some like to be worshipped with tulasi or bel or basanga leaf and flowers such as hibiscus, bluebell, yellow oleander or the lotus; some love to be served flesh and blood in a skull, some love to eat cakes, porridge or flavoured rice, some gorge on fruits while some others relish fried fragments of rice, parched rice and puffed rice. They all ride different vehicles such as elephant, horse, donkey, mule, bull, peacock, swan, crane, owl, parrot, snake, crocodile or other reptiles. For weapons, they hold a sword, a stick, a bow, a discus, a rope or a hook.

To please the gods, the Odias write poems and sing paeans, dance, and play the instruments, the women draw patterns with rice flour paste, prepare hued cotton strings with knots on them (each knot is tied for the well-being of family members) and wear them on the neck or the hand, cover their bodies with cloths having the deities' names written on them, and even inscribe their names on the walls of the house. Doing all this, the Odia man or woman feels safe and secure. Lastly, the Odia woman keeps a fast on behalf of her family to please her beloved deity. People from all walks of life and of every station are offered rights to worship a separate deity.

To dismiss these rituals as unnecessary or meaningless is foolish. Every osha and the accompanying ritual embodies a belief system in a particular social context and gives expression to the cultural sensibilities of contemporary times. It is true rituals are man-made and may appear anachronistic yet in the observance of these rituals is a deep-seated legitimate desire for good life.

Jatra and its types

The region of south Odisha has always been a fertile ground for experiments in the jatra form. In the older days, there were several popular forms of jatra among which some, such as Harikatha,

Naga: Sahijata, Puri

Dandanata, Kandheinata, Ramalila, Dasakathi, Radhaprema lila, Bharata lila, Deshiya nata and Prahlad nataka continue to thrive. As these performances travelled both from the court to the public spaces and vice-versa, they acquired new shapes and forms as they came to be associated with different religious beliefs and customs and were performed with the accompaniment of different styles of dance and music.

Prahlad nataka

Ramakrushna Chhotray, the erstwhile king of Jalantar in south Odisha, is believed to have 'created' Prahlad nataka [A play on Prahlad]. The cast comprises common men and women and hence is called *loka nataka*. The script of the play, inspired by the Sanskrit drama tradition, is based on the stories of *Vishnu Purana* and *Nrusingha Purana*. Most interestingly, the characters speak in local inflections of several languages such as Farsi, Urdu, Hindi, Bengali, Telugu and Odia. Besides Chhotray, several others such as Kishore Chandra Jagaddeb (king of Surangi), Padmanabh Narayan Deb (king of Paralakhemundi), Ramachandra Shuradeo (king of Tarala), and Bishwa Bihari Khadanga have written plays based on the story of Prahlad. Over time, this musical dance drama which was being performed in royal courts has travelled out to the public space such as the village ground.

The scene and setting of Prahlad nataka is the court of Hiranyakashipu, who is a Siva devotee and

Hiranyakashipu: Prahlad Nataka

Hiranya and his queen

has conquered the three worlds. The stage is set up on the village grounds and is prepared in seven layers to depict the seven spheres of earth, heaven and beyond. Much care is taken to choose the actor for the role of the demon king for he has to carry the weight of a large crown on his head and go around with face thickly painted in red. As he takes long strides across the stage, one is reminded of Kansa of Dhanujatra and Ravana of *Ramlila*. The circular movements of Prahlad dancing in space transports the audience to another world. The crowns of Hiranyakashipu and Prahlad are the other main attractions of this play.

    Prahlad nataka is not a mere play but becomes a part of life of the villagers who begin to see the Lord in Nrusingha as he tears away with his long nails the flesh of Hiranyakshipu. No one in the village eats non-vegetarian food on the day on which the play is performed. Every Saturday the villagers worship the mask of Nrusingha.

Scholars often draw parallels between Prahlad nataka and Yakshagana of Karnataka because the musical composition of the former has similarities with Carnatic music. It is true that there are several examples of overlaps between Odishan and the southern traditions of musical performances. However, while an artist Shivram Karanth of the south has infused new life and vigour into the traditional yakshagana performance, Prahlad nataka languishes in oblivion.

Radhakrishna lila

Radhakrishna lila first caught popular imagination with Jayadeva's *Gitagovinda*. Chaitanya's advent in Odisha gave a philosophical turn to the idea of lila. Later, with the accompaniment of dance, music and songs, lila

Prahlad

acquired a whole new art form and began to be performed for the entertainment of people. Pandals, temporary and permanent, were erected in mathas, temples, village grounds for the performance of Radhakrishna lila. As philosophical narratives about Radha and Krishna traversed the length and breadth of the country through saints and philosophers such as Madhva, Nimbarka and Vallabhacharya in the south and Surdas and Mirabai in the west and north, the southern region of Odisha gradually became the site for experimenting with the philosophy of the south and the performance traditions of the north. As a result, in 1868, a new form of lila takes birth in the court of the Chikiti king, which becomes known as *Radhaprema lila*. The *lila* is said to have been composed by the king of Chikiti Kishorechandra Rajendra. However the real author is the father of Kishorechandra, King Viswambar. It is said that the king took the help of the court poet Hanuman Raiguru in composing the *lila*. The lila is made up of around eighty four songs to be sung in eighteen ragas, some of which are ashadhashukla, bangalashree, chakrakeli etc. The cast comprises 23 characters including Radha, Krishna and their friends.

There is an interesting story behind the birth of this form of lila. After marriage, the prince Kishorechandra for some reason desisted from getting intimate with his new wife which worried his father King Viswambar. The King thinks of ways to bring his son and daughter-in-law closer. Taking the help of his poet, he started composing a lila with Radha and Krishna in mind. A Vrindavan-like set is created in the court premises and the new bride and the prince are made to act as Radha and Krishna. Gradually, during the course of the act, love blooms and the two come together as a couple. The earthly relationship is transformed into a divine union which enthrals the audience and the king is happy.

In the nineteenth century the lila, patronised by the royal

families of Dharakot and Ghumusar, travels to various parts of the region. Rural actors take upon themselves to propagate this art form; new songs are composed; the songs of the Vaishnava poets too enrich the performance. All compositions, however, bear the name of Kishorechandra. In the beginning, the cast comprised mainly young actors but gradually older experienced actors began to perform in the lila. Radhakrishnaprema lila may be accepted as the proto-variety of *râsa* or *gitabhinaya*.

An equally popular provincial form of dance-drama is Bharata lila inspired by the Mahabharata. The birth of this cycle of performance plays is commonly traced to fifteenth century—at the time it was popularly called "Subhadra harana suanga"—but it has not been possible to trace its roots to any particular region of Odisha. The origin of the suanga form itself is a matter of conjecture. However, as the cycle of plays traveled through space and time, it took various names such as

Huguli Bharata, Bhadikila Nata, Duari Nata, and eventually Bharata lila. The last two names are believed to have originated in the nineteenth century; the name Duari nata was given by one Shyamasundar Sabat of a village called Kandhakharida near Hinjulikatu. Among the well-known composers of Bharata lila are Kabichandra Jogindra, Srinibas Das, Bhima Panda, Sibaram Sahu and Birabar Sahu.

In the story, Subhadra falls in love with Arjuna who is not moved by Subhadra's declarations of love and simply refuses to marry her. Krishna, however, would see to it that Arjuna marries Subhadra. How everything comes round to the end desired by Krishna is the subject matter of Bharata lila. Creative imagination conjures up an image in the name of Duari who would make it happen. The artists of south Odisha bring into form a unique character called Duari whose ensemble is a curious blend of the attire of people from different parts of the country. He is dressed in kurta and a flimsy cotton jacket on top of it, and breeches. The shirt is decorated with a bronze majel. On his body are drawn dots of various colours. He wears two different colours on the sides of his face and a pointed cap on his head. He has grey beard and wears beaded necklace and ankle-bells. He holds a walking stick made of kendu branch. The audience is mesmerised by his presence on stage.

Duari is a natural poet, well-versed in Sanskrit. By way of advising Subhadra, Satyabhama and Arjuna, Duari comments on social practices and familial responsibilities. At the same time he does not forget to comment on illicit love even as he tries to bring home the point that love is truth. Duari is no other than Krishna.

Bharata lila is a perfect blend of dance, music and performance. The verses are sung in *chhanda* and *chaupadi* forms. Although Bharata lila troupes have dwindled in size, yet several artists such as Nabaghana Parida, Shatrughna Swain, Sannyasi

Behera and Santosh Padhi have done their best to keep this traditional art form alive.

Another art form which flourished concomitantly in Paralakhemundi and in the Odisha-Andhra border regions is *Hari nata* or *Hari katha*. The description of Hari's lilas is the main purpose of this performance. The cast and crew comprises just about two actors and a singer, a dancer, a drum artist and a one-man chorus. At present only three groups in Paralakhemundi continue to perform *Hari katha* but they are well on the path to oblivion.

Scholars have attributed the flourishing of these art forms in the southern region of Odisha to the failure of the state in satisfying the political and social aspirations of its subjects. The state, in order to divert people's attention from the political vacuum, went on an overdrive to patronise varied art forms. The pervasive popularity of lila, however, has dwindled over the years.

'I am Kansa': Dhanuyatra of Bargarh

Journey without end: Bargarh Dhanujatra

Amapalli is situated on the bank of Jira river flowing by Bargarh town. This region is famous for Dhanujatra, the performance of which started in 1948. Since then every year the jatra is held for 11 days starting from the fourth day of the bright fortnight of Pausha. The nature of the jatra and its performance, obviously, has changed drastically over the years.

The tradition of Dhanujatra derives from a well-known story about Kansa and his reign of terror. Krishna was born of Kansa's sister in a prison of Mathura and had been secretly transported to a village named Gopapura opposite the Yamuna to grow up and return to kill Kansa. Kansa who had received ominous signs about his impending death, tried various ways and means to have the baby Krishna killed. In the course of all this, the king cries and laughs out of fear. Dhanujatra, in fact, is famous for the laugh of Kansa. It is Kansa's laugh which draws audiences from all over the state every year. Kansa tries out everything within his means to have the baby killed but fails. He then sends Akrura to fetch Krishna to Mathura for Dhanujatra. The king also invites Nanda and the villagers to witness the jatra as well as the fall of Krishna as Kansa envisaged. However, it is Kansa who falls dead at Krishna's feet but not before acknowledging the truth of Krishna. Over the ages, poets have portrayed the event as a *lila* of Krishna.

This story has been there everywhere: purana, kavya, mahakavya. However, it is the lila form that has endured. The 'sanchar' group had once been an important medium for Krishna lila. In Bargarh there used to be competitions among the sanchar groups. Later, sanchar artists started Krishna jatra, performing the various episodes, beginning from the marriage of Vasudev and Devaki to the death of Kansa, in different places of Bargarh. Ambapali and Bargarh turned into Gopapura and Mathura respectively. Large podiums were created in playgrounds, on riverbanks, inside mango forests, near the temple, inside the weekly village market, on the streets etc. and the cast was picked up from various places. The past was no more thought as distant, it was enacted and perceived in the present. There occurred complete identification of the audience with the characters and their trials and tribulations.

The nature of performance of Dhanujatra in Bargarh is not, as some say, a recent development but a modern form of an ancient mode of performance initiated by various religious communities including the Jains, the Buddhists, the Christians, the Vaishnavas as can be seen in the performances of Krishna lila, Ramalila, Shivalila held in Mathura, Brindavan, Varanasi, and in several places in south India. However, the Dhanujatra of Bargarh is planned well in advance and relatively more organised. It is to be kept in mind that in this jatra it is Kansa who always has had the most drawing power.

The Kansa of Dhanujatra is the emperor of the world. He is a philosopher, poet and scholar, a polyglot, well-versed in the shastras and a connoisseur of the arts. His court plays host to philosophers and artists from all over the region. He loves and is loved by his subjects and is forever mindful of their welfare. He has put in place a well laid-out system of justice. In his dialogues, interspersed with his famous inimitable laugh, Kansa draws examples from various parts of the world and their governments as well as from history to warn rulers against repeating the mistakes of the past, holding the audience spell-bound. The emperor is a gracious host as he receives guests and ambassadors from all over the world. Yet in the middle of all this, he is sometimes overridden with an emptiness and a feeling of loss, for he has not yet met Krishna.

The last act: Krishna and Balaram with the dead body of Kansa

Ramalila

In our cultural experience Ram represents all that is good and worthy of imitation. His life and behaviour is the gold standard for a son, a husband, a brother, a father, and, a king. It was not without reason that Gandhi envisioned India as *Ramrajya*. As is true of all great epics, the nature of the characters of *Ramayana* takes different forms as the story travels across time and space. Even the character of Rama acquires different hues of behaviour. As a result, we now have over a thousand Ramayanas across Asia and South-east Asia.

Valmiki's Ramayana was born out of a specific socio-cultural and political context. The idea of *Ramarajya*, however has gripped political imagination across time and space; Rama represents the highest standards of religion, class and community, and thus has been transformed to a universal ideal. As a result, every religious community has a Ramayana of its own. The Jainas have Jaina Ramayana: among the sixty-two arihantas in the Jaina traditions, Rama is one. Rama is also an important figure in Theravada

Buddhism as well as in the Buddhist Dasaratha Jataka, and, is an enduring character in the religious texts of the Vaishnavas, the Shaivas, the Shaktas and the Sauras. Rama has been variously understood as *nirguna* (Kamban's *Ramayana* and Tulasi Das's *Ramayana*) and *saguna brahm,* and, is the central character in *Yogavasistha Ramayana, Adhyatma Ramayana, Devi Bhagavat, Adbhuta Ramayana, Mahabharata, Bhagavat Mahapurana, Maharamayana, Mantra Ramayana, Agnivesha Ramayana, Shambhu Ramayana, Duranta Ramayana, Shravana Ramayana* etc. One also finds compositions such as Rasika Ramayana and Ramayana for dalits. In Kamban's Ramayana, Mahi Ravana asks Ravana if he had made love to Sita, to which Ravana replies: "One can make love to Sita only in the form of Rama. But the moment I appear in front of her in Rama's form, I am overcome with feelings of kindness, righteousness, forgiveness and peace, and I find myself turning away from Sita." In fact, Rama's character is very powerful.

In Odisha, Rama and Ramayana arrived first through the

Ram and Lakshman: A Madhubani painting

medium of architecture. Various characters and scenes from the Ramayana such as Rama, Sita, Surpanakha, Maricha, Jatayu, Bali, the construction of the footbridge to Lanka, the killing of Bali, the kidnapping of Sita, the meeting of Rama and Sugriva, the archery exploits of Lakshmana, Lakshmana being injured by Indrajita's Shakti weapon etc. have been depicted in great detail in several temples across Odisha such as Shatrughneswar temple (6th c.), Swarnajaleswar temple (8th c.), Singhanath temple (10th c.) on the bank of the Mahanadi near Bhubaneswar, Barahi temple (9th c.) in Chaurasia, Sun temple of Konark (13th c.), Ananta Basudev temple (14th c.) in Bhubaneswar and Somnath temple, Bishnupur (15th c.). Mutal paintings depicting scenes from the *Ramayana* are also found in ancient temples such as Jagannath temple, Puri, as well as on the walls of Gangamatha of Manikarnika sahi, Puri. The murals on the walls of Biranchinarayan temple, Buguda,

Ram, Sita, Hanuman and others: Raja Ravi Varma's painting

Ramlila of Bishipada

Ram, Sita and Lakshman in Panchabati: Ravi Varma's painting

Angad in Ramlila of Bishipada

the Srikurma temple on the Odisha-Andhra border named Srikurma, and the Jagannath temple of Dharakot as well as the ancient pattachitra paintings in palm leaf manuscripts of *Adhyatma Ramayana, Baidehisha bilasa* prove the popularity of the story of Rama in the Odisha region.

Obviously, Odisha too, like other regions, has its fair share of Ramayanas and Valmikis. There are two Ramayanas — *Bichitra Ramayana* and *Bilanka Ramayana* — believed to have been composed by Sarala Das. Whether Sidheswar Das is another name for Sarala Das is still being debated. The former Ramayana is the earliest composition in an eastern Indian language and is written in the compositional style of *smrti katha*. *Bichitra Ramayana* has been edited by Sachidanand Mishra and translated into Telugu. Here Sita is portrayed as one who questions the patriarchal social structure. In *Bilanka Ramayana* the poet highlights the exertions of Sita and the virility and valour of Rama. The poet of these Ramayanas is undoubtedly one who had read Valmiki's Ramayana and questioned his creativity and written the Odia Ramayana as an original and

Bali

independent text. The voice of resistance in these Ramayanas is reflected in Balaram Das's *Jagamohan Ramayana*. The author, daringly, questions the deeply entrenched social and political structures of the day. Inspired by Ramanand, Balaram even transforms Jagannath into Rama and, in the vein of Rasika Ramayana goes on to portray the love between Rama and Sita and the beauty of Nature in an imaginative and aesthetic manner. Balaram's composition has inspired later middle era Odia poets such as Arjun Das (*Rama bibaha*), Dhananjay (*Ragunath bilasa*), Upendra Bhanja (*Baidehisha bilasa*), Tripurari (*Ramakrushna Kelikallola*), which in turn have popularised Rama's character and life as an ideal to be emulated. In the later period, several *chautisha*s were based on the ideals of Rama. At a later stage, the performance of *rama lila* across the length and breadth of the region have established 'Rama nama' in the popular imagination as the mantra of salvation.

Sugriva in Ramlila of Asureswar

Shabari and Ram-Lakshman

O Mountains, O Trees…

'O Mountains, O Trees, my loving husband went to hunt a deer'. 'Sitting on the branch of Shingshapa tree, Hanu says to himself…' "Tell me Hanu, 'How is my lord, how is Lakshmana'", 'Hearing the news from his minister, the twenty-armed Ravana leaves in anger on his Pushpaka vimana'. There is hardly anyone in Odisha who hasn't heard these lines from *Rama lila*. It is almost impossible to describe the deep emotional impact that these lines have on the audience. The songs are sung in various metres and ragas. The bare musical accompaniments include a mridanga, mardala, khani, dasakathi and a pair of small cymbals. Sometimes, one hears the harmonium too.

The stage is generally set in the village grounds or in the temple premises, or in the mango grove or near the river bank. One ought to witness, at least once, the Rama lila performed at Asureswar, Dasapalla, Bishipada, Nayagarh, Bhanjanagar, Boudh etc. In Asureswar, it is quite a sight when Rama and Lakshman ride a chariot from Lord Raghunath Temple to the Jagannath temple, covering a distance of about 1.5 km Jagannath temple is decked out as Janaka's palace; it is where the marriage of Rama and Sita is solemnised. People gather in thousands to watch Rama as a groom and participate in the marriage party amid the blaring music of the band party, sankirtana and fireworks. In Dasapalla, Rama goes to the forests to hunt a rhino. A wide road becomes the scene of war between Rama and Ravana. Arrows fly past as men, dressed as soldiers. Swords are brandished and maces used. In Bishipada, the large village field is turned into Lanka, where men wearing masks of bears and monkeys keep jostling and gorging on fruits in the shops nearby till Hanuman arrives and sets Lanka on fire. Ravana, Kumbhakarna and Indrajit get inside three separate huge hollow tree trunks to put up a mesmerising act. Their hand and head movements are controlled by other actors. In Boudh, an islet inside the Mahanadi becomes Lanka and the town is turned into Ayodhya. In Bhanjanagar, the images of Rama and Lakshmana used to be taken in a chariot to the

The coronation of Ram

place of performance. With Rama lila troupes in every village and town, the entire region of Odisha goes back, as it were, to the ancient days when Rama walked the face of the earth.

Hanuman, Vibhishana and Ram

Rama, it is said, arrived in Jagannath temple in Puri and became a part of the Odia religious culture through the preachings of saint Ramananda in the thirteenth century. Balaram Das, it is believed, composed his Ramayana in the precincts of the Jagannath temple. The report (1805) of Charles Groom, a British colonial officer, describes the performance of Ramakatha inside the temple. However, it is Upendra Bhanja's *Lavanyabati* which first mentions the dramatic tradition of *Ramakatha*. In the poem, the king of Karnata sends an artist couple to Singhala to perform *Rama katha* so as to make Lavanyabati fall in love with Chandrabhanu. The

Ram, Sita and Lakshman on their way to the forest

performance is in the mode of a shadow play. In Odisha, *Rama katha* takes the form of drama when in the eighteenth century Biswanath Khuntia rewrites the epic as a poetic drama. His composition called *Bichitra Ramayana* made the poet a popular figure among Odias who affectionately called him Bishi. Bishi Khuntia's Ramayana inspired numerous compositions in the later period and Rama joined Krishna as the beloved hero of the lila form of entertainment in the Odia-speaking regions.

The festival of Rama lila acquires a distinct character in the temple town of Puri where the celebrations begin on Ram Navami and go on for eleven days. It is the time of *sahi jata*, when several plays are performed in different localities across Puri. Groom's report mentions several jatras performed during those days: Rama jhulana jatra, Rushyashringa jatra, Janma jatra, Jagar jatra, Bibaha jatra, Banabasa jatra, Maya mriga jatra, Lankapodi jatra, Ravana badha jatra and Ramabhisheka jatra.

Vashist and Sriram

For the plays, the characters are drawn from among the local residents of Puri.

Rama lila was once a highly popular form of entertainment in the princely states such as Bhanjanagar, Dasapalla, Nayagarh, Phulbani, Boudh, Sonepur, Sambalpur, Badamba, Athagarh as well as in Mughalbandi areas such as Asureswar, Kendrapara, Cuttack and Puri. The kings of these areas constructed Rama temples adjoining their capitals and provided patronage to Rama lila performances.

The life and character of Rama, it seems, provided a sense of comfort and security during a period of cultural and political vacuum created during the colonial rule. The British masters became, as it were, the representatives of Ravana. The people of south Odisha have always been loyal to their kings and were a formidable force against the British. This probably could have been the reason for the popularity of Rama lila performances.

It is said that the tradition of Rama lila travelled to Odisha from Banaras, where it started in 1625 when Narayan Das, the favourite disciple of Tulasi Das, dramatized *Ramcharitmanas* into a play. However, it is in 1805 that Udit Narayan Singh, the Maharaja of Ramnagar, Banaras, gave it a distinct form. Given the cultural and religious ties between Puri and Banaras, it may have been that the Rama lila tradition of Odisha was influenced by the Banaras tradition in great measure but we cannot deny the fact that prior to it *Ramakatha* was alive in different art forms that were exhibited in Odisha.

The lost world of puppets

Everyone in this world is either a puppet in another's hands or has made others his or her puppet. In the Odia worldview, we are a world of puppets. According to Jagannath Das's *Bhagabata*, we are puppets in the hands of the Lord who makes us dance with the triple threads of triguna. Imitating the lord, we make the puppets dance out our innermost feelings and desires. Besides, the puppets can be made to enact all that is impossible to be enacted by human actors on the stage. Naturally, puppetry was one of the most popular forms of entertainment in the past.

Puppets are of several kinds: those which are made to dance on fingers, those controlled by threads, those which dance with sticks and there are those whose shadows become characters. In Odisha, these puppets respectively are known by different names: *sakhikandhei, gopa lila kandhei, rama lila kandhei* and *ravana chhaya*. The performances of *sakhikandhei* and *gopa lila kandhei* are based on Radhakrishna lila. The stories of the latter two are those of Rama lila. In the past, puppetry was a medium of entertainment, education and the dissemination of social and religious ideals. Puppets were even used in psychotherapy.

In Odisha, puppetry was the vocation of people from the lower social class. The artists of *sakhi kandhei* and *gopa lila kandhei* belonged to the *kela* community, those of *ravana chhaya* came from *bhata* group, and the artists of *kathi kandhei* were of the *jhara* community. Puppet artists in other parts of India also generally belong to the lower social class. The Kelas are nomads. However, as artists the puppeteers were the most popular entertainers at village fairs and festivals. Presently in Odisha, the number of puppetry artists has dwindled; for example, there are only two groups of *sakhi kandhei* in Mantripada of Kendrapada district, two groups of *ravana chhaya* artists in Kutarimunda village of Odasha in Anugul district and just around three groups of *rama lila kandhei* artists in Kendujhar. The artists no more hail from the traditional community of artists but belong to the upper

Sakhi Kandhei of Mantripada

Ravana Chhaya

castes. However, *sakhi kandhei* continued to flourish, thanks to the efforts of the artists from Bhanjanagar, who started a movement of sorts in the 1940s. They gradually brought more artists into their fold and *sakhi kandhei* gained popularity in several places such as Rajkund, Sanakodanda, Nayagarh, Dhenkanal, Raidihi, Kalibiri, Badamba, Athagarh and Kamakshyanagar. By 1970s, there were around 50 groups from Badakodanda, Rajkund and Raidihi who used to perform at different places of the state. They put up stiff competition against the opera groups. They used to sing chaupadi, champu, odishi, bhajans and janana, and even performed magic tricks. Puppetry started to decline in the 1980s as the artists migrated or left for more lucrative occupations. Even then, they continued to perform on demand. Scholars provide accounts of how *ravana chhaya* had travelled to south-east Asia and have hailed it as an old form of cinema. Today, the puppets lie shut in wooden boxes or trunks or are on display in museums as relics of a long-lost past and puppetry is described as an art form of the dalits even though puppet shows are being organised in schools, colleges and hospitals.

The goddesses of Odisha and the rural carnival

Come Chaitra Purnima, it is time for the carnivalesque celebrations of Jhamu jata of Kakatpur, Thakurani jatra of Brahmapur and Hingula jatra of Talcher. On the riverbank or on the village ground, one may see the brisk dancing of the kaibarta covered in a horse-shaped bamboo frame wrapped in colourful pieces of cloth while others play the bugle and the drum. The song goes thus: 'First I worshipped Ma Baseli and then Haragouri...' The performers narrate stories with the help of proverbs and puzzles; elsewhere competitions are held between the horse dance groups. The *patuas* [devotees] of goddesses Sarala and Mangala, dressed in long red blouse and a colourful skirt walk on wooden stilts, carrying an idol of the goddess, decked with garlands of red hibiscus, in their arms, and an oil lamp fixed to a wooden post on their heads which are wrapped in red-coloured cloth. Along with them are some attendants playing the cymbals. Some *patuas* themselves play the cymbals and dance, drawing throngs of villagers who excitedly welcome the *patuas* and bow down to the goddess and finally see off the *patuas* with generous alms.

For *jhamu jata*, long pits are dug in rows and filled with burning coal which glow frightening red as incensed resin is sprinkled over the embers. The devotees, called "poda patua" walk over the embers without the slightest expression of pain. Elsewhere, one sees "phoda patua" pricking their tongue with iron nails or going around a bamboo pole with one end of an iron chain tied to it and the sharp end of the chain dug into the flesh on the back. Onlookers close their eyes in extreme fear as they imagine the pain tearing into their flesh. One might ask if it is necessary to inflict such pain upon oneself. However, these patuas believe that such austerity and the tolerance of immense pain would drive out the feeling of self-importance and instil a feeling of surrender before the goddess. The devotees are all too anxious to pass the test.

These goddesses of Odisha — Bimalai, Tarini, Narayani, Mangala, Sarala, Hingula, Charchika, Ramchandi, Gadchandi, Basulei, Bajramahakali, Ketuka, Chhinnamasta, Dhumabati — occupy a supremely powerful position in the Odia mind and heart. All the goddesses love red flowers and love to wear red or black sarees. Some are fierce-looking while others have a benign beauty. Some love to be offered flesh, meat or fish while others would have nothing but grains and pulses. They ride various kinds of animals such as donkey, goat or a pig. Their dwelling place is often under a tree or a small thatched hut at the main end of the village. They sit there in rain and sun guarding the well-being of the village. Anyone, irrespective of class and caste, is free to worship them. The Mother accepts all that is offered with love and devotion. However, anyone who is filled with pride and pretence is bound to incur the wrath of the goddess.

Danda nata

Shiva is an interesting figure, a curious mix of opposites; he is both a householder and an ascetic, always dependent on Shakti yet has conquered his senses, his body is smeared with ashes yet is endearingly attractive. He loves to be worshipped with pinwheel and datura flowers and bel leaves, wears a snake around his neck, covers his waist with tiger skin, holds a trishula in one hand and a dambaru (a kind of tambour) in another, and rides a bull. His special attributes are that he is a member of the lowly caste, a farmer, a nomad, a poet, a dancer, is a man of great wisdom and is omniscient. His wife is Mahashakti, his beloved and supreme yogin.

In the month of Baisakha when the skies are clean and clear and the sun's rays pierce the skin and the earth is too hot, human beings feel the need for the benevolent presence of Shiva and Shakti on earth. So many yogis have spent their lives, using various means to satisfy Shiva and seek his blessings. Some lie buried in heaps of snow, some enter the fire, some stand on one foot, some keep their heads down and legs up as austere forms of   penance to earn Shiva's appreciation. There goes a story that once a devotee, in anger, tried to pour a basket of dried fish on Shiva because the latter wouldn't listen to his prayers. Shiva halted him and gave him what he wanted. Some even say Shiva is always addicted to smoking ganja. Why do people say such things about a nomad like him? Why do householders find him so endearing? Is it because deep within, all of us are ascetics, lone souls? Is it possible to reject this world and its pleasures? Can we discard all trappings and live an egoless life? If yes, we need to rise up to the level of Shiva consciousness, if no, we need to pay our respects to such an entity.

The Odia Dandanata is expressive of affection and respect for Shiva. It all started when thirteen rishis, including Vashishtha, Atri and Angira, realised that they needed to propagate Shiva consciousness among earthly beings. Each donned a single ochre-coloured robe and left behind his knowledge, philosophy and ego in the ashram and went out among other human beings. It was summer season on earth. The rishis gathered in a Shiva temple and gave up their earthly name and clan and called themselves Shiva gotri (members of the Saivite clan). With a holy staff in one hand and a fire-lamp in another, they went around for thirteen days preaching universal brotherhood and peace and invited householders to live the life of an ascetic for just thirteen days during which their souls would undergo transformation, before they returned to worldly life. Dandanata is the performative expression of this thirteen-day penance.

In rural Odisha, there would gather at least thirteen devotees called *dandua*, irrespective of class and caste, in a Shiva temple. After lighting a lamp and worshipping the holy urn, the devotees start touring villages to preach the greatness of Shiva. One of them performs the role of *pata bhokta* (main actor), others are called *bhokta*. The troupe includes other devotees and musicians. Some villagers, who hold a fast for thirteen days, invite the dandua troupe who perform a silent play in which they give dramatic representation of the tradition of agriculture, from sowing to reaping the harvest. At night, they cook their own food, relish *pana* [a drink made of banana and bel juice mixed with bhanga] and rest under a tree before they start again at daybreak to perform *danda nata*. The play performed on the village ground is called *dhuli danda*; that which is performed inside the pond is called *pani danda*. The festival ends with mountain worship on the day of Baisakha sankranti.

In the street at night, a stage is set. It is sprinkled with holy water and the idol is worshipped before the play (*dandanata*) begins. The characters — the sweeper and his wife, Shiva and Parvati, a saura and his wife, the fowler and his wife, the washerman and his wife, the yogi and his wife, the harpist and his wife, and, a jester — arrive one after another. The jester is a wise man who provides the commentary and metaphysical interpretations of various social issues. Every character acts out his own problems and the solutions are given by the mahayogi, Shiva. The play is scripted by one from among the villagers. There are some variations in subject and theme as we go from village to village. Dandanata has changed over the years, making it a living form of art, but its basic qualities have not changed.

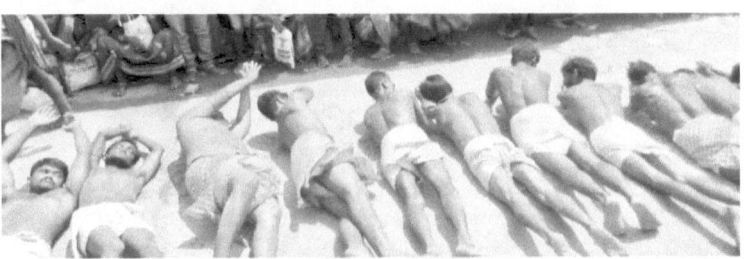

A performance ritual of Dhulidanda

Pala: May there be no suffering, 'Hari Hari Bol'

'Pala', some say is derived from 'palyate', or 'panchali'. Several others have explained it as apabhramsa form of 'paryaya'. However, we generally use the word to denote a scene of heated verbal exchange driven by attempts for one-upmanship and is filled with criticism, judgement, mockery, sarcasm, scoffing and much jibing. The Odia *pala* begins with one group initiating a discussion accompanied with musical instruments, dance and scholarship. Questions are asked by another group. In the charade that follows, the nuances of the subject being debated are laid bare. The scene becomes more interesting when more groups join the debate. As the groups debate and fight the audience joys in those debates and fights.

Pala is a celebratory worship of Satyapir — a joint representation of Satyanarayan, a Hindu deity, and Pir, a Muslim saint — and, thus, propagates the message of communal harmony. The greatness of Satyanarayan is described in four chapters of "Reva" canto of *Skanda Purana*. It is his story that constitutes the subject of Pala. Pir is a saint whom the Muslims worship seeking the fulfilment of their desires. However, the story of Satyapir began to take shape out of the peaceful co-existence of Hindus and Muslims when Mujauddin Mohammad Khan was the subedar of the region. Today, Satyapir is worshipped in the Odia household to celebrate the birthday of a child until he or she is sixteen years old. What is called the idol stand is a small wooden stool. On it the priest places a piece of red cloth on which are placed the five deities, Ganesha, Narayana, Rudra, Ambika and Bhaskar. Five betel leaves are placed on the four corners and at the centre of the stand. A betel nut and a banana are placed on the leaf in the centre. Four strands of peacock feathers are placed upright besides the four corners of the stool. The strands are decked with flower and tulsi garlands. As offering, the householder prepares *sirni*, which is made of mashed bananas, jaggery and milk. All family members sit down to hear the story of Satyapir when the priest reads out a chapter from a book of *shohala pala* [sixteen episodes of pala] whose author is said to be

A scene of Pala

Kabikarna. Sometimes, the priest's attendants repeat the lines in sing-song voice, holding the listeners in rapture. As this pala is performed with the reciters and the listeners seated, it is called *basa pala*.

For all Odias, Satyapir is none other than Jagannath. *Pala*, therefore, is a unique expression of the Odia cultural psyche. While Kabikarna has divided *pala* into sixteen episodes, Kunjabihari Dash describes twenty-six episodes of *Satyapirpala*, all of which comprise *baithaki pala* or *pothi pala*.

Sometimes, families organise a *thia pala* in which the reciters perform an all-night show which is attended by the whole village. The composition is generally multilingual comprising Urdu, Odia, Bengali and Sanskrit. The sound of cymbals and mridanga and *hulahuli* [inarticulate sound made by women by wagging their tongues] reverberate in the air as the performers narrate stories from puranas and upanishads to preach peaceful co-existence and communal harmony. The master narrator is uniquely dressed. His costume includes silk kurta and pyjamas or dhoti, a long piece of cloth which hangs down his left shoulder, and a turban, big-sized earrings. He holds a chowrie and waves it on and off as he and his attendants chant a high-pitched "Hari Hari bol" to mark the beginning and end of a discussion as also to mark a change of pace in the narration. The master narrator is known for his knowledge of the shastras and his interpretations and commentaries offer simple practical solutions to the problems of life because of which he is highly revered by the people. Among the well-known *pala* artists are Lokanath Kar, Harinath, Niranjan Kar, Jagannath Behera, Paramananda Sharan, Niranjan Panda, Biswanath Patajoshi and Baishnab Pradhan. These artists and many more have successfully incorporated changes in the subject matter of *pala* performances making it a thriving form of art even today.

Yama, Sabitri and Satyavan: A painting by Raja Ravi Varma

Sabitri brata: A story of love, death and immortality

On a no-moon day in the month of Jyeshtha, Sabitri walks past the dark and dense earthly sphere to try and force Yama to give back her husband's life. In the words of Aurobindo, Sabitri's silent journey is the story of a profound evolution of humankind.

As it was then, so it is now. Every married Odia woman waits for someone to arrive from her parental home. The messenger would bring with him her parents' blessings and all that she would need — fruits, bangles, sindoor, a few pieces of turmeric root, a pint of kajal, lac-dye for the feet and a new saree — for the ritual worship of Sabitri. And, if it is the first year of marriage, there would be various kinds of sweetmeat and several other countless things to tug at her heart and remind her of the days she spent as a child with her parents. For the rituals, she takes a grinding stone and dresses it as Sabitri, lights the diya and incense, gives fruits as offerings, reads the *Sabitribratakatha* which has the story as it occurs in *Skanda Purana* and *Bhavishya Purana*. The story, in short, goes thus: King Aswapati fails to find a groom for his daughter Satyavati who dazzles all with her beauty and intelligence. The men are intimidated and wouldn't dare to seek her hand in marriage. Aswapati, therefore, asks Satyavati to choose a groom for herself and the princess sets out on a chariot. She travels the length and breadth of her father's kingdom before she comes across a handsome man in the forest. He is prince Satyavan, whose father is the blind king Dyumatsena who has been ousted from his throne by usurpers. Sabitri tells her father about her decision to marry Satyavan. However, Satyavan is fated to die just after a year of marriage. On the fateful day, Sabitri, aware of Satyavan's impending death, accompanies her husband who goes out to fetch firewood from the forest. After a few hours of work, Satyavan feels weak and tired and lies down with his head in Sabitri's lap. Immediately after, Yama the god of death arrives to

The worship of Sabitri in Odisha

take away Satyavan's soul. Sabitri follows Yama and pleads with him for her husband's life. On the way, she answers Yama's questions. Yama is pleased with her devotion and steadfastness and tells Sabitri to seek boons. Eventually, Sabitri wins back her husband's life and the well-being of her family.

It is almost clear that this story was the outcome of a patriarchal structure which obligated women to bear the responsibility of the family's well-being. Aurobindo, however, represents Sabitri as a manifestation of the Supreme Consciousness, who incarnated to dispel the darkness of ignorance and lead humankind to its spiritual destiny. Every occasion of *Sabitri brata* thus is a silent reminder of the immense potential that a woman carries within her.

Ritual offerings

Yama

Satyavana and Sabitri

Lalita *pala*

Lalita endears to the Odia imagination like no one does. If it weren't for her and her love, Vidyapati would never have found trace of Nilamadhaba. It is no wonder that her story has been the theme of numerous dances, songs and cinema. However, in the countryside, it is *Lalita pala* which rules the roost. The *pala* was born out of the imagination of Odia and Bengali poets who lived in the border regions of Odisha adjoining Bengal. In Odisha, it is a popular form of entertainment in Bhogarai, Jaleswar, Chandaneswar and neighbouring areas. Though called *pala*, it shares less similarity with *Satyapir pala*, as described earlier, and is more a *suanga* performance. But, like *Satyapir pala*, it does represent conflicts between different religions and beliefs. No clear solutions emerge. The drama is in the conflict. Like pala, Lalita pala is multilingual comprising Odia and Bengali languages in the least.

The story of Lalita, which began to circulate in the fifteenth century, has its origins in "Vishnu khanda" of *Skanda Purana*, and *Purushottam Mahatmya*. However, in these sources there are Indradyumna, Viswabasu and Vidyapati but no Lalita. When Lalita appears later in time there occurs a confluence of cultures and traditions leading to the dramatic discovery of Nilamadhaba and the subsequent birth of Jagannath, the most powerful symbol of religious and communal harmony.

It is not known for sure who the composers of *Lalita pala* are. One would get further details if the manuscripts currently in the possession of gurus and masters are compiled and edited. However, Lalita pala, as it exists now, is based on the manuscripts in the possession of Krupasindhu of Arapihar in Jaleswar and Bijayagobinda Das of Shonitapuri in Medinipur. The acting style is a mixed form of gitabhinaya, suanga, and Sanskrit drama. The act begins with a dialogue between Shuka and Parikshita, in the puranic mode. Parikshita, terrified of his impending death in the hands of Takshak seeks to hear from Shuka the story of Purushottama Kshetra and Jagannath so as to earn salvation after death. The dialogues of other characters are a mix of prose and verse. The scenes are interspersed with songs, dance and music. The musical accompaniments include harmonium, flute, tabla, cymbals and mridanga. The setting is a village in Bengal, where Lalita resides. Lalita's songs are in Bengali whereas the songs of Vidayapati, who is a foreigner, are in Odia. Two minor characters Gopal Singh and Netua speak in a mix of Urdu, Hindi and Odia. The use of multiple languages clearly represents the real-life language mix in the speech of people who live in border regions.

A bamboo swing in Raja festival

Raja parba: Let the mind soar

At the end of Jyeshtha and the beginning of Ashadha, when the parched earth is anxious to receive the first drops of rain, the village girls sit on a swing and push the ground with their feet to fly as high as they can, as if to invite the clouds to rain down on earth. 'Let the mind soar…Let it touch the clouds and come back', they say. It is that time of the year, when the farmers bide their time before the feverish activities of the agricultural season begin. Mother Earth would have to bear immense pain when the sharp ploughshare strikes deep to loosen her up. Therefore, when she menstruates at this time of the year, she needs to be taken care of. Women and girls take care not to tread on her too much. They, therefore, take rest from all household work for three days, play on swings, and relax, while the menfolk spend the three days playing cards and resting. The fourth day of Earth's menstruation is *Basumati snana*, when she is smeared with turmeric and given a ritual bath. The farmer keeps ready a new wooden stool, new clothes, turmeric, the grinding stone, the ploughshare, sandalwood, vermilion and several other things needed for the worship ritual. All this is to seek Earth's blessings for a bountiful harvest as well as to seek forgiveness from her for having to dig and turn the soil for sowing. However, with growing urbanisation and reduced agricultural land, much of the flavour of *Raja* celebrations is lost.

Raja was once a time of joyous celebration when unmarried girls, dressed up as little brides, took to the swing to rise and fly and sing "The swing is heavy and about to break…I can see the crown shining on my brother's head." As the bamboo swing goes high up, the girls sing: "As long as you are here, you are our own, O daughter / Cross the threshold, you belong to us no more." These *Raja* songs speak of the trials and tribulations of a married woman's life and create an air of melancholy for the unmarried girl who realises that she would soon leave her carefree life at her father's home for a life of responsibilities. While the girls play on the swings the boys and men are busy playing cards, ludo and snake and ladder. Everyone is seen chewing on *Raja pana*, betel leaf mixed with scented lime and betel nut and a host of other mouth-fresheners and the smell of freshly cooked rice

Children enjoy on the swing

cakes and sweet porridge wafts in the air. Gipsy women call out to the women inside the house to have their arms tattooed and try out new colourful bangles while snake-charmers lay open their bamboo cases and play the flute to invite one and all to witness snake dance.

Rajasankranti is celebrated on *Mithuna Sankranti*, the day Sun leaves the second sign of the Zodiac cycle Vrishabha to enter the third sign Mithuna. Mithuna is represented as the joint image of a man holding a mace, and a woman holding a *veena*. Various communities across the world celebrate the time of the year when summer ends and the rains are due for arrival, but, according to the folklorist Chakradhar Mohapatra, the festival of Raja is exclusive to Odisha. According to Prithvi Sukta of Atharvaveda, the Earth which is home to all beings, is to be revered and worshipped. *Raja*, thus, is a celebratory expression of the spirit of reverence for Mother Earth.

Swing and soar

Thiadoli: Stand and soar

Dasakathia:
'Chant the holy name of Rama'

Gayaka: *Chant the holy name of Rama...he who is Janaki Ballabh, Naveen sundar and Ghanashyam. The Patta-nayaka who is as good as his father and is also father-like to his subjects is Naveen, beautiful and Ghanashyam, and, the land of Odisha is the holiest of all.*'

No sooner does the gayaka [master narrator] finish his introductory lines than the *palia* [assistant] shouts at him to stop: *Hey Madhu! What nonsense is this! This is a stage not an election platform! This is the stage of Lord Rama. The audience would blacken our faces, do you understand?*

Gayaka: *Brother, even you misunderstood me! I thought you were a wise man. However, I am sorry, I will never ever utter Ramachandra's name. And yes, let this day be the last day of our friendship.*

Palia: *Please let it go. Why don't you explain?*

Gayaka: *Okay, listen now. If I commit mistakes, pull me by the ear. But if you interrupt me, I will rub chillies on you,*

Andhra chillies, remember. So, who is Ramachandra's wife? Janaki. Am I not right? So what would you call Ramachandra? Janaki Ballabha. Swami [husband], as you know, is also called Ballabha. Now, wouldn't you call Ramachandra Naveen sundar for he is forever beautiful? Besides, the colour of his skin is like that of the blue sky. Is it not? That explains Ghana-shyama. Who is called nayaka? Who is the nayaka among us? Nayaka is the king or the head of a clan. Patta-nayaka is the chief among kings. Let us continue. What kind of a man was Ramachandra's father Dasharatha? He was brave, enjoyed great respect, had many wives...Ramachandra, however, married only once.

Palia: *Hey Madhu, let us talk about Ramachandra. Our subject is the death of Ravana. Let us sing the story of Rama — the one who is forever beautiful; the one whose skin is blue in colour; the one who brings death to the wicked; the one who will bring death to that fellow Agadhu Sahoo — come, let's continue...*

Such goes the narration in dasakathia in which the narrator

Dasakathia

and the one-man chorus hold the audience spellbound as they recite lines from the epics, shastras and puranas set to the tune of two rectangular pieces of black wood which they keep slapping against their palm, and comment on the socio-political order of the day with varied facial expressions and a flourish. The sharp clap which accompanies the recital conveys a bone-deep understanding of Odia life and struggles. The art form is believed to have originated in Ganjam amid the bitterness of communal conflicts among Hindus and Muslims. Folklorists have been able to trace Agadhu Sahoo (19th c.) of Khandara village in Hinjilikatu area as the original composer of dasakathia. Some others push back the origins of dasakathia to mid-17th century. Yet others, citing the Ramayana, believe it is an ancient art form; they give examples of how Vishvakarma prepared a set of

Ojhapali of Assam

Dasakathia of Odisha

wood clappers for Lakshmana to keep the soldiers entertained. Even Hanuman is said to have had played the clappers while chanting the name of his lord, Rama. Both Hanuman and Lakshmana are the *dasa* (servants) of Rama. Therefore, it is perhaps easy to see why the instrument is called dasakathia; infused as the performance is with Rama-consciousness, some also call it 'ramatali'. According to another account of the origins of dasakathia, there used to be a nomadic tribe in Ganjam called *dasira* in and around the eighteenth century. The *dasis* used to go around playing the clappers and begging for alms. Rama and Krishna were the main heroes of their stories which were gradually accepted among the common folk and the tribe was assimilated into caste Hindu society. Today, there exist several dasakathia groups in Cuttack, Puri and Dhenkanal besides Ganjam.

Dasakathia composition comprises episodes such as Ashvamedha yajna, Lakshmi purana, Nala Damayanti, Nilendri harana, the battle between Rama and Hanuman, the killing of Mahiravana, Icchhabati harana, Shobhabati harana, Radhakrishna

Dasakathia performance

milana, Kartika mahatmya and others. The songs have lines of fourteen letters and the master reciter sometimes interjects with chaupadis in metrical variations.

There are only two characters in dasakathia performance, the narrator and the one-man chorus. Their costume includes silk dhoti and kurta, an uttari [light upper garment], a black coat and a tailed turban. They wear a Ramanandi mark on the forehead, big-sized earrings, a silver locket, and, bells on their feet. Like the pala artists, the dasakathia artists are spontaneous poets, and possess excellent acting and musical skills.

The stories revolve around three themes — elopement, surrender, and death — and are filled with shringara, veera and karuna rasa. The audience rolls with laughter and rages in anger at the same time as the artists, with detachment, quote the shastras and draw examples from all over the world to illustrate their statements. The audience is struck by their wisdom and deep awareness of the cultural situation.

Among the artists who have contributed greatly to the popularisation of this art are Krushnachandra and Baidyanath Rathasharma, who was awarded by the President of India, and his assistant Bhimsen Satpathy. Other well-known master narrators are Kashinath Panda, Adikanda Padhi, Ananta Panigrahi, (Gayakabhushan) Upendra Panigrahi, Trinath Padhi, Damodar Mohapatra, Durgacharan Mohanty, Udayanath Sahoo, Krushnacharan Satpathy, Paban Charan Swain, Ramahari Padhi, Muralidhar Bisoi et al. Thanks to the form and format of dasakathia, the artists have been able to incorporate traditional and contemporary elements in their performances making it a flourishing form of art.

Mogul Tamsa:
Beware! Here comes Mirza Sahib!

'Stand up in silence; Stand aside!' the chopdar calls out. All stand up to greet Mirza sahib, the Mogul ruler, as he arrives with royal flourish and climbs up the platform to occupy his throne. The servitors such as *bhestiwala, jhaduwala, pharras, hukkawala, pankhawala, daftar, chutneywala, toti* and *bardar*, show up one after another to mark their attendance. They are followed by the jester, a yogi, *madhu, piada*, zamindar, and a cowherd woman. Mirza sahib shows his displeasure with the zamindar who has failed to collect the desired revenue and *chhokri, bakri, chhapar khat, masuri, bepasham* and other *rasad* [goods]. The performance which is widely held in Bhadrak, is a popular form of entertainment even today.

Mogul Tamsa owes its origins to farcical performances of yesteryears such as *lila* and *suanga*. Some scholars have tried to trace its origin to the Tamasha form of art in Maharashtra. The first author of Tamasha (tamsa) is said to be a brahmin, Ram

Joshi (1762-1812). The Maratha rulers Baji Rao II and Wajid Ali Shah II are said to have provided patronage to tamasha which gradually underwent change in form and character to include actors from all strata of society.

The author of Mogul Tamsa is a brahmin named Bansiballabh Goswami who lived in Sangat village of Bhadrak. Born to Satyanarayan and Satyavati, Bansiballabh was of spiritual nature. It is said he once met a Bhil sanyasi who blessed him with great learning and wisdom, after which Bansiballabh started writing tamsa plays and earned wide fame such that he was acclaimed in the Mughal court. The tamsa plays written by Goswami are Bhil tamsa, Radha Krishna tamsa, Chehoda tamsa, Jogi tamsa, Phakir tamsa, Lolin Majabai tamsa and Mogul tamsa. The then Mogul ruler granted him a piece of land, a pair of gold earrings and a turban. The piece of land, as it exists today, is known as *mogul dihi* or *mogul chaka*.

The tamsa plays, which used to be performed in the month of Chaitra after Shivaratri for days together until *Pana sankranti*, are collectively called Chaiti tamsa. The association of Shiva with tamsa is perhaps because of its origins in Maharashatra where Shiva was the state deity.

Cowherd woman and Mirza Saheb

Mogul Tamsa is unique because of the use of multiple languages: the mirza speaks only Farsi while the servitors speak a mix of Farsi, Hindi, Urdu, Bengali and Odia. The zamindar, the *gumasta* and the cowherd woman speak only Odia. Farsi was the state language of Odisha during Maratha and Mughal rule, and was in wide use even during the British rule, up till 1838.

Mirza

The open-air stage is set generally in the premises of a Shiva temple. Musical instruments include the drum, harmonium, tabla, pakhawaj, kubuji, violin and sitar. The play is a farcical enactment of popular derision against the mirza's luxurious life-style, biased judgements and lust for women and power. The characters of mirza and the zamindar remind one of Dildar Mian and the landlord Ramchandra Mangaraj of Fakir Mohan Senapati's novel *Chha Mana Atha Guntha*.

Mirza Saheb among dancers

Mirza Saheb and his courtiers

Discovering Odia Culture | 105

The dear little sister who craved for a few broken grains of rice
(The story of Khudurukuni)

It is that time of the year when, after the rains, soft white cottony clouds float across the clear blue sky and the rivers, having calmed down, shimmer in the sunlight. The bright yellow flowers of the ridge gourd and cucumber plant dance in the wind while squirrels scurry for the paddy grains stored somewhere. Young joyful girls get busy, setting up the stage for the worship of their beloved goddess Khudurukuni for she would bless and protect their brothers.

Once upon a time there was a little girl called Ta'poi, the one and only beloved sister of seven sea merchants, who would do anything for her. Bereft of the cradling arms of her parents who died while preparing a silver moon for her, she became a daughter for her brothers' wives, who loved and cared for her. Everything changed after a jealous brahmin widow started poisoning the women's minds. In the absence of the seven brothers who had gone abroad with their merchandise, Ta'poi was sent away to the jungle to mind the goats. She was hurled into a dark rat-infested room which became her home and her days passed in such great hunger that she craved even for *khuda*, [a few broken grains of rice]. In great sorrow, she sought the protection of goddess Mangala. Her brothers returned soon after and found her in the jungle where they heard her sad story. They brought her back home and decided to teach their wives a lesson. When the men reached home, their wives came out to welcome them. 'Where is Ta'poi?' the brothers asked. The women said Ta'poi isn't at home. The men immediately cut off the nose of all women with the knife in Ta'poi's hand, except that of the youngest, Nilendri. The women rushed to Ta'poi who is overcome with pity and prays to Mangala again. Her sisters-in-law got their nose back and they all lived happily ever after.

Long ago, the region of Odisha was known for its flourishing sea trade, when merchants sailed for far off islands in south east Asia, and, a number of deep seaports such as Palur, Manda, Sippara, Manpur, Dosrun, Kokla, Amarda, Tamralipi came up along the Kalingan coast. Curiously, Ptolemy does not mention Tamralipta (Tamralipi) though these were flourishing seaports even in 600 B.C. One finds fascinating descriptions of nine kinds of sea vessels in *Paikakheda* composed by Champatiraya Chudamani and edited by Sadashiva Rathasharma. The nine kinds are Bahitara, Gandia, Chotamukhi, Surachaturi, Rajpur, Laua, Khaidanga, Gangaprasad and Nadia khudupa. Fakirmohan Senapati mentions the name of three vessels — Gorapa, Saluka and Du'uni — in the chapter "Baleswari Pangaluna" in his autobiography *Atmacharita*. An old song by the famous singer late Akshay Mohanty also mentions 'Gorapa'. According to Chakradhar Mohapatra's treatise on sea trade "Annababihara", the vessels from Kalinga used to carry elephants, silk clothes, iron tools and several other stuff and animals as well. On return, they brought home spices, silver bricks for making coins and various kinds of precious and semi-precious stones. Besides trading in goods, there was an exchange of languages and cultures. Historians have given detailed accounts of how the sea merchants of Kalinga were responsible for the diffusion of Kalingan culture not only in south-east Asia but also West Asia and even Greece and Rome. The Khandagiri caves, the sculptures of Greek guards, animals with wings, the pillar carved in Indo-Persian style, and carving of the giraffe in Konark temple stand witness to the exchange of cultural traditions among the artists and sculptors of ancient Kalinga and those of Nineph, Babylon and Persepolis.

Every Sunday in the month of Bhadraba the girls wake up before dawn to gather flowers for worship, decorate the walls with rice paste, collect fruits and *khuda* for offerings and clothes and jewellery for the goddess. Khudurukuni is an intimate reminiscence of the strong ties that hold a family together.

The *sadhabas* of Odisha had to travel far and wide in rain, storm and wind. Who else but Shakti could save them? Therefore, the merchants, before every journey, offered their prayers to Mangala and installed an idol of the goddess on the prow of their boats to ward off the evil forces. It is for this reason that young girls celebrating Khudurukuni osha worship the Mother and invoke the power of Shakti to protect their beloved brothers.

Ritual worship of boita

Chhau Dance

The village thunders with the sound of dhol and dhumsa and the stage platform shivers under the forceful thump of the dancers' feet. It is as if 'the dancer is one with the dance'; there is hardly any one in the audience who would look away while chhau dance is on. This martial dance form originated and flourished in Mayurbhanj and in the adjoining areas such as Purulia in West Bengal and Sarheikala in Bihar.

Trying to explain the name of the dance form, scholars have identified 'chhak' as the essential dance pose of chhau in which a variety of gestures are made by using six different parts of the body. They are *dabana daba, hanthu pharaka, kamar kasha, chhati chhita, baha thesa and ghencha saja*. Besides, there are six kinds of movements in the dance, six different variations of tempo, six different masks, six kinds of songs such as *judan, baithaki, pandashalia, darabari, neg and achar*, and six kinds of *bheda*. Six different cultural communities such as kudmi, kumbhar [potter], kamar [blacksmith], mochi [cobbler], domb [sweeper] and badhei [carpenter] are represented but the songs mostly describe the daily activities of a woman of the kudmi community. The name 'chhau', therefore, may have been derived from the Kudumali word for six. There is use of six different musical instruments such as *dhol, mahuri,* flute, *chadchadi, madala,* and *dhumsa.*

There are other opinions too about chhau. Some say chhau form originated from the use of three props — *chhauni* [a tent-like structure], *chhaya* [shadow screen] and *chhadma* [mask]. The chhau of Mayurbhanj has its beginnings in the performances in the king's durbar. According to the popular story, Maharaja Krushnachandra Bhanja once went hunting into the forests and accidentally shot dead a pair of tittiri birds who were by the riverside to quench their thirst. A farmer named Mangat Mahanta, who saw this happen, would not let the king get away with it. He forced the king to regret and acknowledge that he had committed a sin. The king also promised to give up hunting and the maharaja and Mangat turned friends. Mangat invited the king to be his guest who was treated to a sumptuous feast and a spellbinding dance performance called chhau. The king decided to provide support and encouragement to the artists; gurus were appointed and the art form changed for the better.

Chhau is a primitive dance form marked by wild movements in six different tempos such as *sada tabka, teu tabka, uska tabka, muda tabka, lahara tabka* and *dubi tabka*. The music involves a limited number of notes. There are generally three kinds of movements in the dance — straight, circular and serpentine — to imitate the movements of wild life in nature. Among the various forms of chhau, the composition of the raja of Mayurbhanj, "Gangabatarana", is the most important. Ganga comes down from heaven, takes her place in Shiva's matted locks, and from there flows down to the earth and becomes home to numerous reptiles and insects such as snakes, frogs, crocodiles, earthworms etc. The dancers convey the subtlest of natural occurrences such as the sound of rain as it drops down in ponds and rivers, the ripples caused by the blowing of the wind on the still surface of water — this dance movement is called 'lahara' — and, the rising and falling of waves called uska tabka; the dance of the peacock and the tiger are most popular among the audience.

The chhau of Mayurbhanj does not make much use of masks; there is a limited use of masks for the characters depicting birds and animals, and demons. The feelings of courage, anger, satisfaction, peace and affection are conveyed through elaborate facial expressions and body movements. Every feeling is conveyed for a strict duration. The performance ends with 'jhumar' song which enchants and overwhelms the audience.

Chhau, in other regions, is marked by predominant use of masks for gods, demons, human beings, spirits, and divine and semi-divine beings. The masks in Purulia chhau are large-sized and colourful; that of Sarheikala are used only to convey facial expressions. The costume comprises heavy accessories such as *taira* [sola earrings for men], *tairing* [flower ornaments for female characters], *jhulana, kanthi, kuhula* and *kamarkashani* [waist band]. The clothes are white in colour and dyed with red earth.

Over the years, chhau has undergone a change in form, content and costume as professional troupes travel across the world. As more women become part of the troupes, the focus is more on facial expressions and subtle and graceful bodily gestures and less on wild vigorous movements. The stage setting too has undergone a change.

'Sabda nrutya':
Nada and its expressions

Kumbhari is a village in the middle of a forest of mahula, mango and sal trees on the bank of river Jira flowing through Bargarh district. The presiding deity of the village is Brajeshwari, who is worshipped in a symbolic form, in the form of a bouquet of peacock feathers. It is said that the deity was worshipped by Balmiki Debata in his house. Balmiki, at a later time, had her installed as the village deity. In the beginning her temple was a thatched hut but later on was developed into a big temple with a mandap. Several years ago, the small village earned fame as the cultural centre of western Odisha, and was particularly known for the dance form called 'Sabda nrutya', a unique representation of art and philosophy.

According to the Indian philosophical tradition, the universe was created from the energy of sound. Sound is Brahm and the universe is an expression of its creative force, Shakti. The originators of this dance form, perhaps, had realised that the truth can be adequately expressed if there is a right mix of sound and gestures and dance is nothing but a creative expression of sound.

Sabda nrutya was originally called *Sabda-sura-patra*, *sura* being the emotional expression of sound. In the earlier days it was performed in the temple premises and then moved to open-air stage. It is generally performed during dhanu jatra, rama lila and râsa lila. The musicians sit on outside of the stage to play their instruments. The dance begins with an alaap accompanied by music played on harmonium, dhol, mardala, cymbals and ghungroo. The feet are the first to move and footwork is dominated by the toes and not by the heels as in Odisi dance. Slow movements give way to fast-paced dancing. The men are dressed in saffron clothes and the women wear saree. The dancers perform complex body contortions, as in gotipua dance, to form a chain or an urn, or a throne or even a discus.

Tandava is a major element in the performance of œabda nrutya. The performance includes almost twenty types of tandava including Vishnu tandava, Ananda tandava, Bhairava tandava with the song compositions taken from Brahma purana, Bhagavata purana, Markandeya purana, Shiva purana and several other

A dance guru

shastras and kavyas. Ganesha tandava and Vishnu tandava are most popular among the artists. As the dance involves complex body movements, many artists drop out as they grow older and the body turns stiff.

The original composers of this performance are believed to be Balmiki Debata and Nagara Guru. The ancestors of Balmiki had come from Banpur. Nagara is the guru of dakshini, gotipua nata and krishna lila. While Balmiki lived two hundred years ago, Nagara was born in the second decade of twentieth century. Several other indigenous forms of dance flourished in the region when the composers lived and worked and hence the dance is naturally a mix of classical and folk traditions. Unfortunately, Sabda nrutya has not been able to travel beyond its region of origin and is struggling to stay alive.

Dalkhai: An intimate experience of Shakti

Dalkhai is the goddess of fertility and presides over the intimate feminine space called the *kothashala* [threshing floor], a space where only unmarried women and no men are allowed. The 'male gaze' knows only lust and hardly wouldbe able to appreciate the enchantment ofdivine union with Shakti. Therefore, Dalkhai's worship is performed by only unmarried women who celebrate the physical beauty and creative power of the goddess. Only one man is allowed in to sing as a bard of the Dalkhai tradition while the women perform a sexually-charged dance.

The two musical accompaniments include the dhol [drum] and the dhunkel [a new earthen pot]. The dhunkel is played by rubbing the teethed part of a bow on a winnowing bamboo fan placed on the lower end of the pot turned upside down. In southern and western Odisha, Dalkhai is worshipped in the form of a branch of the amla tree. Members of several adivasi communities such as Binjhal, Ganda, Kela, Sabar and low-caste

Hindus such as Gauda and Dom are originally believed to have formulated the ritual practices followed during the worship. In the kothashala during the worship, it is said the spirt of the goddess enters the bodies of some female devotees who are made to smell a branch called 'dahana' as the goddess is believed to love the smell. Overpowered by great sexual energy, the devotees enter a state of trance.

The worship room is either square-shaped or rectangular and measures sixteen units or multiples of sixteen. Sixteen images are drawn of Durga, Parvati, Ishwar, Ahalya, Tulasirani, Narada, tortoise, fish, Hanuman, the 'dahana' branch, Shakambari and other such male and female figures. Nine plants are worshipped as symbolic forms of the goddess. They are: plantain, colocasia, turmeric, jayanti, asoka, bel, masharu, paddy and pomegranate.

Several myths and legends have grown around Dalkhai worship. According to a story which seems to point to the union of adivasi and Hindu traditions, King Nala had a sister named Railabati who had kept a fast for Dalkhai. To convey her satisfaction with Railabati's devotion, Durga threw down from heaven a flower branch which began to be worshipped as a representative of the goddess. As the branch is called 'dala', the worship tradition developed as 'Dalkhai'. Dalkhai is observed on ashtami [eighth day] of the bright fortnight of the month of Ashwina but arrangements for the worship begin on saptami [seventh day] when unmarried girls carry wicker baskets and go to the river ghat. Amid drum beats, the girls worship the seven sister goddesses, Jnanadei malen, Nitai dhuben, Luhukuti luhuren, Sukuti chamaren, Pitei sabaren and Gangi sabaren. The baskets are filled with river sand and brought to the kothashala where seedlings are buried in the sand. A few days later they sprout and then begin to bear flowers. Dalkhai worship thus is a ritual performance in agricultural societies, held in deep reverence

Dalkhai dance

for Mother Earth. After the worship rituals are completed on the navami [ninth day], there starts a carnivalesque night-long programme of song and dance.

Odisha has a long tradition of worship of feminine energy as is evident from the tantra peeth of Patnagarh and Sonepur regions in western Odisha. At Patalapanka in Nuapada district, people have been worshipping a stone which is in the shape of the female genital organ. It carries a curious name called 'Dwarashani'. In Kalahandi and Nuapada one finds several idols of goddesses called by different names such as Dwarashani, Gangadei, Mauli, Ghantashani, Pataneshwari, Dalkhai, Budhima and Babure and several other strange names. These deities are the guardian protectors of the village.

Like Dalkhai, Bhai jiuntia is another festival celebrated with much fanfare in western Odisha. The festival has its origins in a story which goes thus: The princess of Champabati, Aruna, happens to fall in love with the minister's son Madansundar. A

Dalkhai on stage

plan is hatched by the king to have Madansundar killed. When the latter's sister Malati comes to know of it, she prays to Durga to protect her brother, who by the grace of the goddess is saved from being a tiger's prey. Bhai jiuntia [let my brother live long] celebrates a sister's unconditional love for her brother. But while Dalkhai is celebrated by young unmarried women, Bhai jiuntia, like Khudurukuni osha, is celebrated by all women who hold a strict day-long fast.

Dalkhai worship, however, has shifted venue from the traditional kothashala to elaborately designed open air pandals in villages and towns. The traditional instruments of dhol and dhunkel have been replaced with modern musical instruments such as *dhumsa, tasa,* violin, flute, *mahuri,* harmonium, etc. These days the performance is often interspersed with popular Sambalpuri folk songs and both men and women are seen dancing together. In a bid to make Dalkhai widely popular, the traditional footwork too has given way to modern dance steps with the result that Dalkhai no more retains its original flavour.

124 | Discovering Odia Culture

The snake charmer and a song for his snake

In the scorching heat of summer, amid the cuckoo's song and the sweet smell of mango flowers, the whole village listens with rapt attention when the snake charmer sings 'Padmatola' [the song sung by snakecharmers for catching snakes] to the beats of the pellet drum. Young and old alike gather around the snake charmer as he opens his wicker basket, thickly plastered with cow dung, to let out the cobra which rises and spreads out its hood and crawls out of the basket as if in a trance.

The snake has always been a potent cultural and spiritual symbol, and has inspired numerous myths and legends about the deep connection that it shares with human life and experiences. It is this awareness that led human beings to specially worship the snake on Naga chaturthi or Nagal chauthi, the fourth day of the bright fortnight of the month of Kartika. For Nagal chauthi, the kothishala [common threshing floor of the village] is washed and cleaned. In the kothishala is a termite mound. A pair of metal statues of the male and female cobra is placed near the mound for ritual worship. The offerings include various kinds of fruits, five coconuts, sugarcane, cottage cheese and sprouted green grams.

Besides Nagal chauthi, snakes are worshipped everyday in Siva temples. In Eastern India, snakes are worshipped in the name of Manasa, Sarparani or Bhudevi. In India, snake worship is an ancient tradition and was popular even in 6th c. B.C; one finds mention of snake worship in Rig Veda. Naga worship has been described in Ramayana, Mahabharata, and the puranas. At a later stage all major religions adopted snake worship as an essential part of their ritual practices. Naga has been associated with the lives of Narayana, Sankarshan, Krishna, Parshvanath and Buddha.

According to Hindu cosmogony there are three spheres. The upper sphere is inhabited by the gods, the middle by humans and the lowest by serpents [nagas/cobras]. Nagraj or Basuki, the seven hooded serpent, presides over the serpent world; Basuki is the one who balances the earth on his head, and hence is all-powerful. Not only that, even Shiva the mahayogi wears a serpent round his neck and is called Nageshwar or Nagabhushan. It is Basuki which was wound round the great mountain Mandara used as the churning rod during the churning of the ocean of milk (see *samudra manthan* as narrated in *Bhagavata Purana*). It is Basuki again who serves as the bed for Vishnu's *yoga nidra*. Basuki also forms a hood over the head of Parshvanath, the Jaina thirthankara.

According to the puranas, the foremost snake ancestor was born of the union of the sage Kashyapa and his wife Kadru. Arjuna and Ashvatthama of the Mahabharata are known to have married Naga princesses. Naga women are believed to be proficient in witchcraft, beautiful to look at and are devoted wives; they are extremely mindful of any harm which might be caused to their husbands. Several royal dynasties in India consider snakes as their ancestors. For example, the Pallavas of south India and the royal family of Asuragarh in Kalahandi consider themselves as descendants of nagas. In Niali, Odisha, there are inscriptions describing the enmity among the kings of Ganga and Naga dynasty. The northern areas of Koraput, as well as the region of Bastar and Kalahani districts used to be under the control of Naga kings. One finds naga idols in Mathura, Amravati and Peshawar. The Odisha State Museum has idols of Kaliya dalana, Parshvanath and Manasa dating back to seventh century.

The human mind has tried to make sense of the snake in numerous fascinating ways. The snake is a dual representation of good and evil. Historically, the snake symbolises fertility, rebirth and transformation. The Bible represents the snake as Satan who poisons the mind of the first human beings on earth and plunges them into a life that would end in death. The yogic tradition uses the image of the coiled serpent as a representation of kundalini energy residing in a passive state in the human body. Across cultures, however, the snake has served as a symbol of divine consciousness. ■

The snake charmer and his audience

Dancing for the Lord: Sakhi nata, Gotipua, and the devadasi

Sakhi nata is the dramatised representation of the desire for companionship with Self. The songs and gestures of this performance derive greatly from Vaishnava philosophy and its natural tenor of joyous abandonment experienced by a human being on the path to her/his spiritual destiny of uniting with the Supreme friend, Krishna. One finds very young boys, dressed up as girls in finery and dancing to the tune of mahuri, mardala, cymbals, and mridanga as they enact the feelings and emotions of Radha, Krishna and the gopis as friends and lovers in a self-contained world. The Brindavan-like setting and the compositions of the likes of Upendra Bhanja and Kabisurya Baladev Rath hold the audience in raptures.

Sakhi nata is believed to have evolved from the impromptu utterances and gestures of the gurus each of who trained generations of young boys to perform *bandha* [complex and exquisite dance poses], and, who were all part of separate groups, which flourished mainly in southern Odisha. It is not known exactly how the *sakhi pila* or *sangita pila* or *nata pila* of sakhi nata groups came to be called gotipua; perhaps it was in recognition of the young boys performing as girls as well as the *bandha* which forms a crucial part of the gotipua dance form.

The history of gotipua goes far back to around six hundred years. The *bandhas* performed by a group of young boys with highly flexible bodies are several, such as *gagan, dwimukha, torana, sangyana, kshudra, trishula, brubhanga, dambaru, pradipa, chira, nahunia, ekapadia, hansa, shagadi, khai, chakri, charamayura, padmasana* and *mithunashraya*. The poses are inspired by Upendra Bhanja's *Chitrakavya Bandhodaya*. However, the original gotipua performance, as the name implies, was performed by a single young boy who used to sing and dance at the same time. These days the boys do not sing. Modern-day performances are more in the style of acrobatic dance much to the chagrin of old-timers who were once enthralled by the frisson caused by delicate and precise movements which were part of *bandha* in the olden days. The movements today are sexually explicit and exaggerated to cater to popular demand as also because of the need to compete with other art forms.

To explain the early forms of Odissi dance, scholars cite gotipua as well as the mahari dance of yore. The mahari dance is said to have given rise to the devadasi dance of a later period. The devadasi dance is a crucial ritual service performed for the Lord at Jagannath temple, Puri. Only an Odia can imagine this: In deep darkness, at the dead of the night, by the light of a dim lamp, the two huge round eyes, the sharp nose, the red lips and the yellow robes and the *dayana* garland. From within the *garbhagriha*, the sound of the anklets beating against the feet reaches out to the devotee who, in her/his mind's eye, envisions the Lord being entertained by the nightly devotional dance of the devadasi. This ritual which used to be performed in the middle of the night at the Jagannath temple is called *Mahari seva*.

As the minutes go by, the devadasi, overcome with deep devotion and the desire for soulful commingling with the divine, performs vigorous circular movements as if in trance. This particular movement is called 'bhaunri', which forms the first of a series of movements in Mahari dance. In the olden days, the Maharis were women in the service of the Lord, intimately connected as they were with the daily and annual rituals in the worship of Jagannath.

The origin of Mahari ritual may be traced to the male imagination in a patriarchal order in which the woman's life purpose is to take care of a man's needs at every stage of life, from childhood to old age. The devadasi is wedded to the Lord and stays married to Him for life. However, she is also required to perform other roles such as that of a mother, friend and lover. It is therefore that Mahari seva is an important ritual service during Nabakalebar, Ram navami, Janmashtami, Jhulana, Chandan jatra and *chapa*. However it is the daily *Badasinghar seva* [the ritual service before the Lord goes to sleep] which the devadasi awaits to gain an intimate experience of the divine.

Gotipua in an akhada

Makar sankranti, *Pusha punei*, and bond of friendship

It is early Pausha, that time of the year, when after bone chilling winter, humans, animals and birds huddle out to savour the warm glow of the sun, and rural Odisha witnesses a sudden burst of activity. The fields are flush with green and yellow colours of the mustard plants and farmers are busy carrying stacks of harvested paddy to the grain-yards plastered clean with fresh cow dung. In one corner of the yard is a large clay stove which is fed with fuel to boil the paddy before it is husked. In another corner, there is a heap of fire around which young and old alike are seen sitting on their haunches and warming their hands on the fire. One is reminded of the line from the children's book: It is very cold in the month of Pausha / Take care to cover yourself.

The whole of India celebrates Makar Sankranti which is the day the sun begins its northward journey. The days would become longer. In the region of Odisha, especially in the villages of Mayurbhanj and Kendujhar districts, makar sankranti is a community festival, a time for homecoming and large family get-togethers. For the Santhal tribe, makar sankranti marks the beginning of the journey of a life of hunting and gathering. The whole village gathers at the shrine of the village goddess for worship. The village youth get ready with bows and arrows to shoot a target set at a distance. The one who hits the target is chosen as the future leader of the village and carried on shoulders amid the noise of drum beats and much fanfare. During this festival which goes on for three days, everyone is dressed in new clothes and finery, there is a carnival of song and dance while the girls remain busy in the worship of Tusudebi and the immersion procession on the last day of the festival. The villagers also hold ritual worships for the ancestors and the nature around them.

The special preparation which is offered to the deity during makar sankranti is *makar chaula* which is prepared by mixing milled white rice grains, jaggery, sugarcane, milk, cottage cheese, coconut and ghee. This special offering is distributed among family members, friends and neighbours to mark the joy of friendship and togetherness. New friends are made by offering *makar chaula* to one another; these friends remain so for life. Makar sankranti is thus a symbolic celebration of friendship and togetherness which is integral to a rich communal life.

One may trace the origin of the ritual practice of offering *makar chaula* to a story in *Brahmanda Purana*. Dronacharya and his wife, who are childless, are one day visited by none other than Durvasa, the great sage much feared for his wrathful temperament. Drona and his wife take all care to satisfy him with food and rest. Happy with their treatment, Durvasa asks Drona's wife to perform a ritual worship called *dadhi manthan* to be rid of the curse of childlessness. As part of the ritual, (it is said Yashoda had performed this ritual worship to have Krishna as her son), the floors are cleaned and plastered with fresh cow dung and a swastik sign is drawn on which is kept a few grains of whole unpolished grounded rice. Upon it is kept a pot of curd.

The pot is decorated with sindoor, kajal, flower garland and a new silk cloth. The woman, who has been fasting, recites the stories of Krishna lila till midday. The curd inside the pot is churned and the idols of Yashoda and Krishna are kept carefully on the cream. The sun god and the goddess are invoked by the recital of mantras. Eight earthen lamps are kept burning in eight corners of the house and the *makara chaula* mix is offered to the deity. Drona's wife, after performing the rituals with devotion and sincerity, finally conceives and gives birth to the great Ashwathama.

Another ritual practice meant to invoke god's blessings for the birth of a child is followed on maker sankranti by a large number of women who visit the Atri hot water spring near Khordha. Those desirous of a child, after worshipping Lord Hatakeshwara in a shrine nearby, take a dip in the spring to look for holy relics, which are believed to bring for them the good fortune of becoming a mother. Those who find none leave teary-eyed, only to return the following year.

The preparation of makar chaula: A ritual community

The puranic story was perhaps called to account in a later period. Makar sankranti, however, essentially began as a festival of nomadic subsistence communities and later became an integral part of the ritual celebrations of these communities when they settled for an agricultural lifestyle.

Pusha punei [Pausha Purnima] marks the end of harvesting and storing of the newly harvested paddy. It is a day of fun and rest for farmers who had been working tirelessly to bring home the fruits of their labour. The new harvest fosters a sense of well-being all around, there is a feast of delicious dishes in very home, and the villagers commingle for endless sessions of song and dance and fun and frolic.

In the Jagannath temple at Puri, *pushyabhisheka* is celebrated on *pusha punei* in which, after the bathing ceremony of the Lord is performed with hundred and eight urns of holy water, Jagannath is dressed up and worshipped as Rama. During the worship, the temple servitors called *chha mahapatra* hold aloft the parasols and the *mekap* takes position as Hanuman. It is on this day alone that these two groups of temple servitors come together for a ritual. It is said the gods themselves come down to earth to witness the ceremony and to enjoy the darshan of Jagannath as Rama.

Meanwhile, in Bolangir, Kalahandi, Bargarh and Sambalpur, celebrations start almost a week before the day of *pusha punei*. Young boys roam the village streets carrying a bowl into which the village women put in rice and vegetables as gift offerings. The boys sing a song called "chher chhera" while hitting the ground with a stick as a musical accompaniment. There is an interesting story behind this song. It is said, once on *pusha punei*, an old woman ate too many cakes made of rice and paddy husks which upset her stomach and after repeatedly attending to call of nature she almost lost consciousness. Chher chhera is an onomatopoeic expression for acute diarrhoea; *pusha punei* is therefore also called chher chhera parab or the festival that brings diarrhoea. Such naming of the festival warns people that they need to be careful against greed and over-consumption.

On *pusha punei*, new bonds are made for friendship and life-long service. The landlords give away bounties to the servicemen who had been working on their lands throughout the year; and new pacts made for another year of companionship.

Chher chhera also perhaps denotes the cultural practice of maintaining cleanliness and hygiene. It is why perhaps the *chhera pahanra* ritual, in which the king sweeps the floors of the chariot during the Rath Yatra, is so named. According to Gobinda Charan Udgata, the word is derived from Sanskrit 'Charchari' which means festivities. *Pusha punei* is celebrated during a time which heralds the spring season and there occurs a surge in desire for life and sport.

Ghumura and Paika: Of battle sounds and war dance

In the diffused silver shine of the moon, among the undulating hills and their dark forests, one sees half-naked figures rising and falling to the tune of the resonant beats of the ghumura. The bodies move in tandem with the beats, exhibiting behaviours of different birds and animals. At intervals, when the dancer kicks the earth with great force to mark a change in movement, one is overcome with thrill.

The ghumura is a pot whose wide mouth is closed with tightly drawn thick leather. The pot is tied to thick strings of cloth and hung over the shoulder such that the mouth faces upwards. The man wearing the ghumura vigorously strikes the leather cover with fingers of both hands, in an odic celebration of his own manhood and virility. This instrument is widely used among tribal communities during folk performances in Kalahandi, Nuapada, Chhatisgarh, Bastar where it is called ghumri. It is said the instrument was first used by hunters, when they went out in groups in the wild, to strike fear among birds and animals. Later the instrument began to be played during battles to fill the soldiers with feelings of excitement and fearlessness while at the same time to cause fear among enemies. Ghumura was one of several other musical instruments, such as *dhol, madala, dadama, bheri, turi, kahali* and *shinga*, used during war, as is evident from Sarala Das's *Mahabharata* and *Chandi Purana* and Balaram Das's *Ramayana*.

In the coastal areas, a wide-mouthed pot called ghum is used as a vessel to store cereals and pulses. The mouth is covered tightly with straw plastered with cow dung to keep away insects and rodents. The Odia word for a pot-bellied man is ghum-

petia. Elsewhere in Odisha, ghum is also used to denote sleep laziness. The short grunting sounds which a pigeon makes while nesting is called ghumghum.

While earlier, ghumura performance was part of communal life, these days, ghumura is showcased as folk art and is generally performed in urban spaces at sponsored fairs and festivals. Special costume is madetoorder. Ghumura beats now accompany several other folk songs and dances. Several ghumura groups have been duly registered and take part in competitions organised by the state. This naturally has brought in artificial arrangements and improvisations to suit audience demands and taste.

Very similar with Ghumura, in vigour and force, is Paika dance [the dance of a type of foot-soldiers]. In Odisha, there are entire villages of paikas who undergo training in the village boxing and wrestling arena on a daily basis and on some occasions display their performance in front of the villagers. If there is a fair or a festival, the paikas don special costumes comprising turban, a long piece of cloth called *paikachha* especially made and dyed for them, a waistband made of animal leather, breastplate and a round shield. Their weapons are of various kinds: *luga, kantia, saptamuna, bhalimukha, joraguali, kautundi, gopuchhati,*

ardhachandra, banka chhuri, pashupati khanda, mamaka, barchha, trishula, mudgar and the mace, all made from iron. Their weapons also include several kinds of *nali* [country-made guns] such as *shagadia nali, baruda kumpa and thunka nali*. After the fight with weapons, which includes bow and arrows, is over, they begin to wrestle amid drum beats and the sound of trumpets, *turi, bheri, mamaka, nisan*, etc. so as to inspire awe and fear.

    Some of the paikas are foot soldiers whose feet are tied to wooden stilts [*ranapada* or *ranapa*]. As they walk with wide steps, they injure the enemy soldiers. It is said, *ranapa* was used in the beginning to help the soldiers traverse difficult terrain in less time. Yashoda, it is said, used to tie *ranapa* to Krishna's feet so that his feet didn't get pierced by pointed stones and thorns in the jungle. In the olden days, in Odisha, *ranapa* soldiers were much feared and admired for their valour and tactics. Presently, *ranapa* is a martial art dance performed only for entertainment. Some other mock combat acts include *banami* which involves revolving a huge cane wheel or bamboo wheel with great speed. Sometimes fire torches are tied to the wheel and it looks like a revolving wheel of fire. *Banami* is a great draw when it is performed before the chariots on the day of Rath Yatra in Puri.

These war dance forms have inspired several children's games such as *kitikiti, bagudi khela, bagha bakri* and *ganjapa*. However, the desire for one-upmanship and victory, sometimes, takes the form of cruel sport such as cockfight and bullfight. The martial art dance forms are said to have been inspired mostly by animal and bird behaviour. Performances like ghumura and paika are nothing but subtle artistic expressions of conflicts and encounters among people, communities and nation states.

The art of war

Ghoda nata: Hey you clever man! Tell me how many breeds of horses there are...

"On the way I killed a boa... At night I make the *chaiti* horse dance and in the day I make beaten rice flakes." In warm summer evenings of the month of Chaitra, the men sing this Chaiti song while the *rauta*, dressed up like a victorious soldier, rides on horseback. In the front are two men inside horse-frames, trotting like horses. By their side is the *rautani* [the wife of the rauta] who sings, "Hey you clever man! Tell me how many breeds of horses there are...if you can't I will enter the fire". Amid the sounds of dhol and mahuri, this man and woman narrate the story of creation, their coming into being and all other matters of society. They question the social arrangements, narrate their problems and find their own solutions. All compositions are impromptu. The whole village participates in this procession of the *kaibartas*, men and women of the fisherman caste.

In Odisha, the kaibartas are divided into two groups: those who make beaten rice flakes, and those who catch fish. Their life

is closely tied with river, sea and fish. The story begins from when Vishnu is in *yoga nidra* atop a banyan leaf in the ocean at the time of universal destruction. Suddenly the waves rise and Vishnu wakes up from sleep. He rubs behind his ear and from the dirt which comes out he creates a man who is ordered to hold the banyan leaf steady. This man, the first-born on earth is called *kaibarta*, born as he was from Vishnu's *karnamula* (lower extremity of the ear). Unfortunately, the kaibarta, who is on guard, falls asleep for a moment and enters the stomach of Raghaba (a type of sea-fish). Vishnu rescues the kaibarta and gifts him a horse and Vishvakarma is called over to build a boat. Vishnu asks the kaibarta to sail away in the boat along with the horse to Singhala and rule the island as Kaibarta king, and worship the horse as Bata shrunga or Baseli, as a representative of the Supreme Mother, the protector of all creation. The kaibarta begins a glorious rule; the horse dies after a few years and, subsequently, is transformed to represent the force of Shakti.

The connection between the kaibarta caste and the horse also has its origin in a story in Vyasa's Mahabharata. Vyasa, as is known, is the son of the daughter of a kaibarta king. It all happened when sage Parashar fell in love with Matsyagandha the kaibarta's daughter and Vyasa was born. As a child, Vyasa wanted a horse as playmate. With his spiritual powers, Parashar his father created a powerful horse and gifted it to Vyasa. Over time, the horse came to symbolise the power and influence of the kaibarta king and began to be worshipped as their guardian deity Baseli.

Baseli is one among the many forms of Shakti. In Puri she is worshipped as Ashvamukhi [the horse-faced goddess]; in Balasore she is worshipped as Kanchakhai; elsewhere she is worshipped as Harchandi, Bimala, Charchika, Ramchandi, and Narayani. Her seat of worship is generally on the bank of a river or at the bend of the river, or on the prow of the boat. Baseli, it is believed, would lead man safely across the river of life. The horse dance is performed in various other regions of the country: in Andhra Pradesh and Tamil Nadu it is called *parashi arbam*, in Gujarat it is called *keli*, in Bihar *basuli nach*. In all these regions the performance is led by the kaibartas who sing the *chaiti* song in praise of Shakti.

Tika Gobindachandra: Do you chant or not the holy name of Rama?

In Baisakha, while it is raining fire, in the shade of the village bamboo grove, a solitary dove sings to the baby dove who has fallen dead: 'Our grain baskets are all full, come my baby, wake up'. Just then the melancholic strain of the *kendera* pierces the air and a new bride in one house and a widowed mother in another peep out through their small windows. The story of Mukuta Dei the queen mother and the ninety-nine young wives of prince Gobindachandra makes their hearts bleed.

Gobindachandra, it is said, renounced the world and it was none other than his mother who instigated him to do so. The jogis (yogis) of Odisha hold whole villages in thrall when they roam the countryside in quiet summer afternoons, singing the story of Gobindachandra. "Tika Gobindachandra" was composed by Daibajna Bipra in the eighteenth century. A similar song in a loftier kavya style called "Gita Gobindachandra" had been composed by Jasobanta Das in the eighteenth century. The story of the young prince who renounced the world circulates not only in Odisha but also in Bengal, Assam, Rajasthan, Punjab and in south India. The Bengali compositions are variously titled as "The Song of Mayanabati", "Goraksha Vijaya", "The Song of Gobindachandra" and "The Song of Gopichand". The last one is perhaps the earliest composition and probably originated in east Bengal region (now in Bangladesh). One may say so because the birth place of the protagonist of the story is in modern-day Bangladesh. Different compositions of the same story by Durlabh Mallik, Mohammad Jayasi and Lakshman Singh are popular in northern and western India. There are palm leaf manuscripts in Odisha, carrying more compositions such as the ones by Chandrasekhar Das (Sekhar Das) and Uddhab Das.

The Odia story goes thus: Mukuta Dei is the first among many wives of King Ripuchandra. Even after years of marriage, the couple is childless. The king, disappointed and frustrated, sends away Mukuta Dei to a jungle where she finds herself alone and helpless. She sends news to her parents and her father who is a king builds a palace for her and sends an army of servants to take care of her. A few months later, Ripuchandra, who is hunting in the jungle discovers the palace and is shocked to find Mukuta Dei living in full glory and splendour. Surely the queen must have taken to sinful ways, Ripuchandra thinks and questions her. Mukuta Dei takes several tests such as walking on sharp iron nails and on the edge of the sword, entering and coming out of the fire unscathed, to prove that she is a *sati*. The king, filled with remorse for having treated Mukuta Dei unjustly, brings her back to the palace and she is honoured with the title of "Patta mahadei" [the principal queen]. A few months later the queen gives birth to Gobindachandra.

Gobindachandra enjoys wordly pleasures only until the age

of twenty-one. Soon after, he is forced by his mother to don ochre-coloured robe and smear his body with ash and carry a begging bowl to leave home and become a yogi as she apprehends his death at this age. Mukuta Dei, through her great spiritual powers, had learnt that Gobindachandra would live only for twenty-one years. She decided she would make her son abandon the physical pleasures of worldly life at the age of twenty-one to go through a yogic journey of control and detachment to gain immortality and infinite peace. Gobindachandra is left under the tutelage of Guru Hadipa, a man of weaver caste.

Gobindachandra's wives, silently, curse their mother-in-law for having brought them into helplessness but Mukuta Dei would not budge. A yogin herself and the disciple of none other than Gorekhnath, she would have nothing but her son defeat death and not become a victim of death.

Under Hadipa's training, Gobindachandra learns to override the desires of the body and the mind. The yogi prince gains powers of omniscience and meets Hadipa's guru Tantipa and the first guru Gorekhnath of Natha sect. The yogic journey continues for forty long years before Gobindachandra returns home to his mother and wives, after gaining victory over death. Is the story about the prince's powers? Is it not about the prowess of a spiritually enlightened woman?

It is said, whoever takes birth on this earth is bound to die. Gobindachandra, however, proves this wrong. His journey preaches the transformation of self through self-control and detachment. The body becomes just a vehicle for the expression of consciousness which is by nature boundary-less and limitless. This is the central philosophy of a religious sect called the Nathas. The Nathas are known by several names in different regions of India: the Siddhas, the Kaulas, the Avadhutas, and the Kanphata yogis. Gorekhnath and Matsyendranath are believed to be the founders of this sect. While Gorekhnath is said to be the incarnation of Shiva, Matsyendranath is believed to be the incarnation of Vishnu. In Odisha, they are known by surnames such as Nath, Mishra, Nathsharma, Debsharma, Debnath, and Goswami. Some texts which propound Nath philosophy are *Shiva swarodaya, Gorekh samhita, Saptanga yoga, Shishu veda* (Gorekhnath), *Brahma kundali* (Siddha Saranga), *Parache gita* (Dwarika Das), *Amarkosha gita* and *Saptanga yoga saar*. In Odisha, there are several *mathas* bearing the name of Nath gurus. There are two famous seats of worship of Gorekhnath in Chhapada and Pandar villages of Jagatsinghpur district.

It is said the birthplace of Gorekhnath is a village called Chandrapur on the bank of river Godavari. Matsyendra was born in Nepal. These religious leaders brought about a confluence of religious philosophies of shunyavaad of Buddhism, nirguna sadhana and the Kaulas. Women are not relegated to the backwaters of spiritual and religious practices. As is represented by Mukuta Dei, the woman, unlike in the tradition of Manu, is not the originator of all desires but is ardently desirous of salvation. The world is not dismissed as an illusion, rather is presented as real in which it is the duty of every human being to distinguish between the real and the unreal and, in the process, know oneself, as Mukuta Dei and Gobindachandra did.

Chakulia Panda: As you give, so shall you receive...

You often see them in pairs, wearing white dhoti with the tail cloth tucked in at the back and carrying a circular palm leaf umbrella. There is a *gamchha* and a bowl slung over the shoulder, and they wear elaborate marks of sandalwood paste on the forehead. Sometimes they walk with naked feet while sometimes they wear wooden slippers. No sooner does one of them finish singing a line, the other picks up the tenor of his mate to add another. The women of the village stand ready with bamboo trays filled with grains, pulses and vegetables to be poured into the bowl hanging down from the men's shoulder. These men who roam the villages of Odisha in hot summer afternoons, bringing home the simple truths of life, are called chakulia panda or chakaria panda.

Their songs, comprising stories from puranas and upanishads, Ramayana and Mahabharata, are the common man's digest. They begin with stories about the power of giving [*dana*] and the good fortune which accrues to the giver, giving examples of King Bali from Bamana Purana, Ravana, Shibi, and Karna. Not only that, they also narrate events and happenings from around the world in the form of verses.

The chakulia panda are men of the mendicant Brahmin caste of the Kashyapa clan. They are known by different caste names in different regions of Odisha: Aranyaka or Jha[ua in Garjat regions and Halua in the coastal areas. They are also said to belong to Balabhadra or Shiva clan. They are called chakulia panda, probably because of the circular umbrella they carry or because their poetic compositions remind people of the wheel of time, the rising and falling fortunes of men over the ages. Sarala's *Mahabharata* mentions *chakra bhikhsu* which describes the pandavas roaming the jungles as mendicants during the days they spent in hiding. Evidently, the chakulia pandas of Odisha have their origins in a distant past.

Sometimes the pair performs the story of the meeting between Rama-Parashurama which is a great draw for villagers. The younger of the two is dressed up as Rama, the kshatriya prince; the other is dressed up as Parashurama, the old Brahmin warrior sage. While it is Rama's duty to protect his subjects,

Parashurama has pledged to his father that he would wipe all kshatriyas from the face of earth. Rama and Parashurama indulge in mock combat, and Rama, inspired by the courage and valour of the old sage gradually overpowers Parashurama. The villagers, who are overwhelmed, take care to fill Parashurama's bowl with various kinds of offerings.

In Odisha, the Janughantia brahmins are believed to be representatives of Parashurama. They are worshippers of Rama and belong to well-to-do families. They are concentrated in the regions of Nayagarh, Badamba, Khandapada, Athagarh and other Garjat regions. A king named Janughanta finds mention in Sarala's *Mahabharata*. The king is a siddha yogi and worshipper of sun god, who blesses him to live on throughout Dwapara yuga. It is certainly not possible to say with certainty if there is a link between the Janughantia brahmins and the king Janughanta. But it may be surmised that the Janughantia caste brahmins were the ancestors of the puranic king.

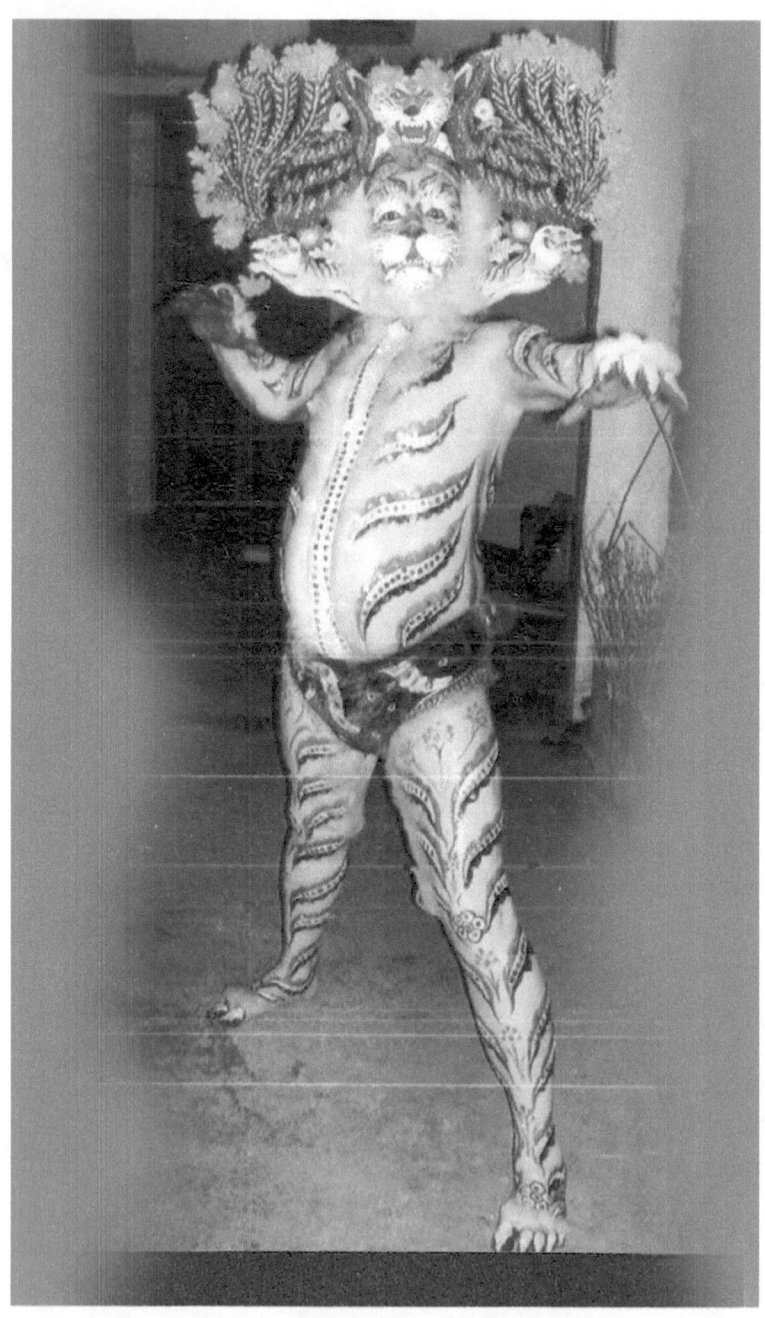

The call of the wild: Tiger dance

If one takes a peek into the green room a few hours before the commencement of the tiger dance, one would see a man shaving his body and painting his body with yellow and black stripes resembling that of a tiger. He then ties a tail to a thick

rope tied tightly around his waist. Finally, he dons a tiger mask, made of organic materials such as wood and paper, and begins to take long strides to walk on to the stage. He is followed by another tiger almost nine to ten feet long and five to six feet high. This one is a tiger frame inside of which are two men to help the huge frame navigate on the stage. Another man inside a tiger frame is dragged on to the stage by a few men. The stage becomes the jungle for all these tigers who move around and sometimes dance excitedly. They hunt, kill and after having their fill, lie down on the stage. The drum beats and the sounds of *changu* and *mahuri* accompanying the whole act heightens the excitement on stage.

This primitive dance form is now an integral part of festivities during Dussehra and other village fairs. The tiger mask is worshipped and the power of the goddess invoked before the performance begins, for it needs great energy and power to be and behave a tiger. It is why perhaps, in some villages of Odisha, the goddess is worshipped as *Byaghra debi* [tiger goddess].

What could be the reason for the popularity of such a dance

form? Is it because it gives us an opportunity to enact our wild desires? Or, is it to express the essential connection between all forms of life? The tiger, in Odia culture, is the object of much love and affection, and is thus called "bagha mamu" or tiger uncle. The story of Tuan Tuin, a couple, who fool the tiger into losing its teeth inspires sympathy towards the tiger. The kindness of a hungry tiger towards its prey *baula* cow is a popular lore often recited by children and adults alike. The tiger dance of Odisha is a celebratory expression of endearment towards the lord of the jungle.

Go slow, O palanquin bearers...for there is a little bride inside: The Odia song of Lament

"Be careful, there is a pit over there, hakum dhabal...be careful, we are at the edge of the field, hakum dhabal"...The *gauda* [cowherd caste] men shout out to one another as they carry the bride in the palanquin. At intervals the still air of the night is pierced by shrill cries of the village women lamenting the departure of the bride who perhaps would never ever return to her father's house.

In Odisha, in not so recent past, girls used to be married off at a very young age. The poor girl, filled with fear and anxiety, would peep out of her palanquin to see the dark moon which reminds her of golden days of joy she spent in her father's house, on the streets and in the mango grove; these days would never return. How fun-filled were those days when she would wade into the village pond to pluck the lily, play larkish sports with her friends, wander on the village street in the full moon night. Now she would be in a new home among new people who would mark the way she sits and walks and talks. An unknown fear grips her mind; in the midst of all this she dreams of a new life.

Who were these poets who poured their hearts out? "Once up, the palanquin wouldn't be put down, O mother!"; "I can no more see my father's house, O mother!"; "You hurt the cuckoo's pride, O father!" "The neem fruit of Chaita tastes so bitter, O brother!" "You abandoned dear Sita in the forests, O brother!" These women who cried their hearts out were the first poets of this land. These compositions called *kandana gita*, or songs of lament, were among the earliest oral forms of Odia poetry such as *chasa gita, phulabaulabeni gita of Kumar purnima, gomha bahuda gita, raja doli gita, kishori melana gita, mangal boli, bhalukuni gita, puchi khela gita, mela gita, haga hamali, samara boli* etc. Among these, *kandana gita* was most popular. In those days, book pedlars would sell booklets titled *Shashidei Kandana* or *Kandana Lahari*. The books were a must-read for village girls who would take lessons on how to behave and how to cook in their husband's house, and how to lament while leaving the

parents' house. Those practices into which they would settle soon after marriage were the first foundations of Odia tradition and culture.

The songs of lament, composed as they were in the innermost quarters of home and heart, are unfeigned, neither controlled by the demands of high poetry nor tied down by restrictions of grammar. In this new age, these songs, like the white-breasted eagle, is lost time memory.

It is the custom among the women of a certain tribe in Rajasthan to perform a lamentation when there is a death in the village; these women, called *rudali*, are paid to weep during death and distress. In the villages of Odisha, during a death or on the occasion of the girl's departure for her bridal home, women of the neighbourhood used to gather to perform a lamentation. Western literature has a similar poetic form called elegy; however, unlike the elegy which is thoughtfully composed, *kandana* is an impromptu oral composition. According to Dale Spender's *Man Made Language*, in a linguistic universe controlled by men, expression of self by women is unnatural and impossible. Possibly, it is why women expressed themselves through songs of lament.

In a conservative patriarchal society, all that girls needed to learn was cooking and taking care of the household. If she could recite a chapter from *Bhagavata Purana*, she was believed to be ready for marriage. Parents would wash their hands off after the girl left for her bridal home. *Kandana gita* is a poetic expression of the woman's silent despair and resistance. "The day has dawned, and the crow's up...Today is the end of all my happiness, O mothers! When the bride's brother gets ready to leave to leave the house to invite the groom for marriage, she sings thus: "My dear brother, should you go to that evil place Narendrapur? That wicked man would be there along with his soldiers, do not fight with him, O brother!" During the ceremonies performed on the eve of marriage, while the family is busy packing boxes of fruits and sweets to be sent to the groom's house, and the girl is made ready for a ritual bath, the girl cries, "I do not want the gold keys, do not bring near me the water pot, I am not yet ready to take a

bath, O mothers!". When the groom finally arrives amid the noise of crackers and drum beats, she lets out a cry, "Look how Kansa comes, kicking a storm / He will carry me away, O uncle! / Amid the fireworks, look there comes the king of Lanka / Who will steal the beautiful Sita / Her life would be hell, O uncle!" On leaving the threshold of her house, the girl, who is made to perform the death rite of her parents, sings thus: "O mother, if I had been born as a boy, I would have stayed on and taken care of father and mother". Finally, it is time to leave, and the girl lets out a wail, "Where are you all, where are my aunts, O mother! You all turned so cruel, O mother!" The moon in deep sorrow, slips behind the clouds.

Banajaga and the rituals of Nabakalebar

Banajaga, the foremost among all rituals of Nabakalebar, is the ritual journey of the priests who set out to look for *dâru*(neem trees to be felled to make new idols)for the construction of the idols of Jagannath, Balabhadra, Subhadra and Sudarshan. The whole of Odisha follows every movement of the temple priests because it is time again for the Lord of the universe to be born anew. The temple chronicles *Madala Panji* describes Nabakalebar rituals, up to the last detail: The *dâru* should carry certain marks — Jagannath's daru should bear the discus mark, Balabhadra's dâru should have a conch, Subhadra's should have a lotus, that of Sudarshan should have the mark of a mace. The priests are to start in particular directions to look for the dâru; the trees are to be felled in a particular manner; the trees with just one or two or three branches are not be felled; the trunk should be of certain width; the trees should not be in the vicinity of a village; no bird should have nests on the trees; no

five-clawed animal should have rubbed against the trees; the tree should not have lost a branch in wind or storm; the tree should not have been struck by lightning; the tree should carry no burn marks; the tree should be mature and healthy; the tree should be measured by the length of the space between two joints of the carpenter's middle finger.

There are elaborate details of worship rituals to be performed before the carpenters set to work on the dâru, such as the gods who need to be invoked, the directions which the priests have to face for worship etc. More instructions follow for the materials to be used inside the bodies of the images to act as nerves, skin, flesh, blood and bones while giving shape to the idols.

Scholars, trying to explain the specific use of wood for constructing the idols, have traced the origins of Jagannath to an adivasi deity. The famous Odia scholar Satyanarayan Rajguru, has identified in the inscriptions two early names of Jagannath: Sri Purushottam and Sri Jagannath. According to an inscription, dated 10 January 1305, in Simhachalam temple, the deities were installed in Jagannath temple in 1308, three hundred years after the coronation of king Bhanudeva II. Rajguru argues that year 1305 marks the beginning of Nabakalebar rituals as it is when the deities were installed for the first time. But it was in 1590, when king Sri Ramchandra Deb of the Bhoi dynasty, who was selected by Akbar's general Man Singh, undertook to reform the temple administration that Nabakalebar gained popularity. Prior to that, as is widely known, the Muslim general, Kalapahada of East Bengal had carried away the idols and had them burnt on the banks of the Ganges. The half-burnt idols were retrieved by Bisar Mohanty who carried them away to Kujang where the half-burnt 'Brahm' was carefully preserved for worship. Jagannath temple was thus without deities for a long time before Ramchandra Deb I installed new wooden images, for which he was called the second Indradyumna, as cited in *Madala Panji*.

However the routine worship of the four deities started for the first time during the reign of Ananga Bhima Deb III (1211-1238). This historical chronicle is inscribed in stone in the Pataleshwar temple in the premises of the Srimandir.

The word Nabakalebar finds mention in none of these texts composed in thirteenth and fourteenth centuries: *Skanda Purana*, *Niladri Mahodaya* and *Purushottam Mahatmya*. Sarala's *Mahabharata*, however, describes only the construction of the idols. The *Madala Panji* volume edited by Gaganendra Nath Dash describes the rituals of banajaga and the consecration of deities along with the practice of Rajbhoga. According to him, such practices started during the reign of Ramchandra Deb I (1568-86).

The fact that *Madala Panji* carries such details is proof of the ancient nature of Nabakalebar rituals. The earliest record of the complete set of instructions is found in a manuscript of 1793. While the 1805 report (a copy of which is in Odisha State Archives) of the then collector of Puri, Charles Groom, gives elaborate details of the proceedings of Jagannath temple, Himanshu Pattnaik retrieves information about Nabakalebarevent held in the years 1714, 1742, 1752, 1771 and 1790. He also says Nabakalebar was performed during the period of British colonial rule in the years 1809, 1828, 1835 and 1846 and then again in 1855 and 1874. Besides Gromes's report, several other records of the colonial period such as the letter of 1809 by Commissioner T. Pakenham cited in a record of 1828, the reports of Kumudnath Banerjee and Commissioner Metcalfe in 1880 carry details of Nabakalebar rituals, the number of devotees who had arrived from afar at Puri at the time, the arrangements made for public health and hygiene of the devotees as well as transport and lodging, and the amount of grant given by the colonial administration for the festival. *Utkal Dipika* carries details of the festival in its editions of July 1893. The Nabakalebar of 1893 was different because the queen of Puri Suryamani Pattamahadei had ordered, as cost-cutting measure, that only the outer layers of the idols be renewed. The rituals were specially performed by the mahant of Jaganath Ballabha matha, Puri. Later, Nabakalebar was performed in 1912, 1931, 1950, 1969, 1977, 1996 and 2015. Besides *Utkal Dipika*, several other newspapers such as *Nabeen, Sambalpur Hiteishini, Prajatantra* and *Samaja* carried elaborate reports of the outbreak of diseases, financial crises, the activities of the priests, the arrangements made for devotees etc. during the festival. The accident of 1977 for which an inquiry commission called B. K. Patra Commission was instituted found special mention in the newspapers.

After Nabakalebar, the temple town of Puri gets ready for the famous Rath Yatra when the Lord starts his journey to his birth-place in Gundicha Temple, a festival celebrated with great religious fervour by devotees across the world.

Bibliography

Odia
1. Das, Chittaranjan. 2002. *Jagatikaran: Sanskrutika Parichiti*. Brahmapur, Anupam Bharat.
2. Das, Dhiren. 1981. *Odishara Jatara*. Bhubaneswar, Odisha Sangeet Natak Akademi.
3. Das, Nilakantha. 1958. *Odia Bhasha O Sahitya*. Cuttack, New Students' Store.
4. Dash, Gouranga Charan. 1991. *Lokanatya Parampara O Kandhei Nacha*. Cuttack, Friends' Publishers.
5. Kar, Indubhushan. 1979. *Sahitya Samaja O Sanskruti*. Balasore.
6. Mahapatra, Sitakant. 2003. *Sanskruti: Ama Samaya*. Cuttack.
7. Maharana, Surendra Kumar. 1993. *Odishara Baudhha Sanskruti*. Cuttack.
8. Maharana, Surendra Kumar. 1994. *Odishara Sanskruti O Sahityaru Kichhi*. Cuttack.
9. Mishra, Ajay. 2002. *Odia Jatra, Unmesha O Uttarana*. Kalyani Nagar, Cuttack: Akshara.
10. Mishra, Nilamani. 1976. *Prachina Odia Lipi, Bhasha O Sahitya*. Cuttack.
11. Mishra, Prafulla Kumar. 1996. *Purana Parampara O Nabakalebar*. Puri.
12. Mishra, Purna Chandra. 2002. *Bhasha, Sahitya O Sanskruti*. Cuttack.
13. Mishra, Ramachandra. 1988. *Loka Nataka*. Cuttack, Orissa Book Store.
14. Mishra, Satyabadi. 1981. *Bharatiya Sanskrutira Bedha Parikrama*. Cuttack.
15. Mohanty, Brajamohan. 1989. *Odishara Sanskrutika Parampara*. Cuttack.
16. Mohanty, Janaki Ballabh. 1993. *Ama Bharatiya Loka Katha*. Bhubaneswar.
17. Mohanty, Prafulla Kumar. 2000. *Shatabdira Shesha Ankare Bharatiya Sanskruti O Bhagabat Gita*. Bhubaneswar.
18. Mohanty, Sarat Kumar. 2002. *Sanskruti O Apasanskruti*. Cuttack, Agradoot.

19. Mohapatra, Gopinath. 1975. *Sanskruti O Bharatiya Sanskruti*. Bhubaneswar.
20. Mohapatra, Khageswar. 1977. *Odia Lipi O Bhasha*. Cuttack, Friends' Publishers.
21. Nath, Shatrughna. 1959. *Ama Bhasha Bibhaba*. Cuttack.
22. Odisha Cultural Forum. 1978. *Odishara Sanskrutika Itihas*. Bhubaneswar.
23. Padhi, Benimadhab. 1995. *Odishara Sahitya Sanskruti O Dharmadhara*. Bhubaneswar.
24. Panigrahi, Hatakishor. 2005. *Sanskruti Parikrama*. Bhubaneswar.
25. Panigrahi, Krushnachandra. 1994. *Sahitya O Sanskruti*. Cuttack.
26. Patel, Shreesh. 1982. *Sahitya O Sanskruti*. Bhubaneswar.
27. Pattanayak, Pathani. *Sahitya O Sanskruti*. Cuttack.
28. Rajguru, Satyanarayan. 1988. *Odishara Sanskrutika Itihasa Vol. 3*. Bhubaneswar, Orissa Sahitya Akademi.
29. Rajguru, Satyanarayan. 1982. *Odia Bhashara Upabhasha*. Bhubaneswar.
30. Rath, Saratchandra. 1996. *Ama Sanskruti Ama Jiban*. Bhubaneswar.
31. Sahoo, Basudeb. 1979. *Bhasha Bigyanara Ruparekha*. Bhubaneswar.
32. Samal, Baishnab Charan. 1972. *Kala, Sanskruti O Sahitya*. Cuttack.

English
33. Adorno, Theodor. 1991. *The Culture Industry*. London, Basil Blackwell, Routledge.
34. Appadurai, Arjun. 1997. *Modernity At Large: Cultural Dimensions of Globalization*. New Delhi, Oxford.
35. Benjamin, W. 1936/1970. "The Work of Art in the Age of Mechanical Reproduction". In *Illuminations*. London, Fontana.
36. Bhabha, H. K. 1994. *The Location of Culture*. London, Routledge.
37. Clifford, James and Marcus, George E. ed. 1986. *Writing Culture*. Berkeley, University of California Press.
38. E. Porter, Thomas. 1971. *Myth and Modern American Drama*. Ludhiana, Kalyani Publishers.
39. Fanon, Frantz. 1963. "On National Culture". In *The Wretched of the Earth*. New York, Grove Press.

40. Honigmann, John J. 1963. *Understanding Culture*. Calcutta, Oxford and IBH Publications Co. Jordan, G. Weedon, C. 1995. *Cultural Politics*. London, Oxford Press.
41. Kroeber, A. L. 1963. *Configuration of Culture Growth*. Berkeley and Los Angeles, University of California Press.
42. Leavis, F. R. and Thompson, R. 1964. *Culture and Environment*. London, Chatto and Windus.
43. Mohanty, Satya. 2000/2003. "The Epistemic Status of Cultural Identity". In *Identities, Race, Class, Gender, and Nationality. Reclaiming Identity*. Ed. Linda Martin Alcoff and Eduardo Mendieta. Oxford and Berlin: Blackwell Publishing, 2003.
44. Mulhern, Francis. 2000. *Culture/Metaculture*. London, Routledge.
45. Pacey, Arnold. 1983. *Culture of Technology*. London, Basil Blackwell.
46. Raymond, William. 1958. *Culture and Society*. Harmondsworth, Penguin.
47. Robertson, R. 1992. *Globalization, Social Theory and Global Culture*. London.
48. Rustom, Bharucha. 2001/2003. *The Politics of Cultural Practice*. New Delhi, Oxford.
49. Saraswati, Baidyanath. 1996. *Interface of Culture, Identity and Development*. New Delgi, Indira Gandhi National Centre for the Arts.
50. Shaked, Gershon. 1989. "The Play: Gateway to Cultural Dialogue". In Hanna Scolnicov and Peter Holland ed. *The Play Out of Context*. Cambridge University Press.
51. Stourac, Richard and McCreery, Kathleen. 1986. *Theatre as a Weapon*. Routledge Kegan and Paul.
52. Styan, J. L. 1963. *Elements of Drama*. Cambridge.
53. Talal, Asad. 1986. "The Concept of Cultural Translation in British Social Anthropology".In *Writing Culture: The Politics of Ethnography*. Ed. Clifford, J. and Marcus, G. University of California Press.
54. Vatsyayana, Kapila. 1980. *Traditional Indian Theatre*. New Delhi, National Book Trust.
55. Whitfield, George. 1966. *Introduction to Drama*. London, Oxford University Press.

www.ingramcontent.com/pod-product-compliance
Lightning Source LLC
Chambersburg PA
CBHW020415080526
44584CB00014B/1339